002105

His Thoughts Toward Me

His Thoughts Toward Me

Marie Chapian

BETHANY HOUSE PUBLISHERS
MINNEAPOLIS, MINNESOTA 55438
A Division of Bethany Fellowship, Inc.

Published by Bethany House Publishers
A Division of Bethany Fellowship, Inc.
6820 Auto Club Road, Minneapolis, Minnesota 55438

Printed in the United States of America

Library of Congress Cataloging-in-Publication Data

Chapian, Marie.
    His thoughts toward me.

    1. Meditations. I. Title.
BV4832.2.C522   1987   242   87-20854
ISBN 0-87123-962-0

MARIE CHAPIAN, Ph.D., known and loved around the world as an inspirational author and speaker, has written over twenty-five books with translations in thirteen languages. She has received many awards for her writing, including the Evangelical Christian Publishing Association Gold Medallion Award and the *Cornerstone* Book of the Year Award.

Books by Marie Chapian

Children:
Slimming Down and Growing Up

Teens:
Am I the Only One Here With Faded Genes?
Feeling Small/Walking Tall

Biography:
Help Me Remember, Help Me Forget
Of Whom the World Was Not Worthy

Christian Living:
Free To Be Thin
Mothers and Daughters
Telling Yourself the Truth
There's More to Being Thin Than Being Thin
Why Do I Do What I Don't Want to Do?

Devotional:
His Thoughts Toward Me
His Gifts to Me
Making His Heart Glad

Contents

Introduction

When I began writing this book I wanted to allow the Word of God to speak for itself with minimal interference from me. For centuries, Bible scholars have experienced the exquisite flow of the Spirit of God as His voice superseded their own. In any paraphrase, however, the human vocabulary can be heard, and so I share with you here my expression of the loving call of a merciful and compassionate Savior based solely on biblical references. In deliberately focusing on His words of encouragement, which He so richly expresses in Scripture, we hear His voice emphatically yet gently showing us that the true disciple must know the Lord's heart. And that's not a quick or simple task.

Will you take a few moments each day to listen to His gentle, powerful voice speak just to you? The Lord knows your heart and He knows your need. He has said He will guide you with His counsel. He has said He cares about every aspect of your life. It is to these truths I dedicate this work. The voice of the Lord is the mighty storm (Ps. 29:3–9), and His voice is also the still small voice after the storm (1 Kings 19:12). Jesus, our divine

11

Shepherd, tells us that His sheep can hear His voice and His sheep follow Him (John 10:27). He makes His thoughts toward us very clear through His Word.

"I have loved thee with an everlasting love," He explains (Jer. 31:3); "I lay down my life for the sheep" (John 10:15). And in His deep caring, He also exhorts, "I . . . will refine them as silver is refined, and I will try them as gold is tried" (Zech. 13:9). And though we are loved and prized by Him, He in no way gives us undisciplined, slovenly license. Jesus said, "Not every one that saith unto me, Lord, Lord, shall enter into the kingdom of heaven; but he that doeth the will of my Father which is in heaven" (Matt. 7:21).

Before you read these daily devotions, will you please ask the Lord to penetrate your heart with His? Will you ask Him to open your thoughts to His? Hear His voice speaking directly to you and receive His special gems to meet your needs.

Take time to be quiet as you enter His presence. He has a message and a challenge for you.

It is my prayer that you will be inspired to love the Lord deeper and truer, and also that you will understand to an even greater measure the depth and meaning of His thoughts toward you.

Together,
Marie Chapian

Free of Charge

*. . . justified freely by his grace through the
redemption that came by Christ Jesus.*
(Rom. 3:24, NIV)

You have My unmerited favor, and you are saved
    from judgment and destruction.
Not through your own striving
    and not through your own cleverness or goodness,
because grace
        is free of charge.
            You were once so far
                away from Me, but through the blood
                of Christ,
            you have been brought near
                and now you are in the center of My
                heart.
I have many gifts for you:
            Forgiveness
                life that is new and eternal
                    healing, strength
                enthusiasm, purpose and productivity

righteousness and peace in the Holy Spirit
inner peace, contentment, blessings
and joy—
all are My gifts to you.
And what do I expect of you?
Roll your works upon Me; trust Me wholly.
Commit your ways to Me.
Every proud and arrogant thought of the heart is
offensive to Me.
Mercy, truth, love, worship and fidelity are My
delight.
Depart from and avoid evil,
and I will purge iniquity from your heart
in order that I may fill you
and become your life.

Ephesians 2:8, 9; Proverbs 16:6, 3

Listening to My Voice

The sheep that are My own hear and are
listening to My voice, and I know them and
they follow Me.
(John 10:27, Amp. Bible)

I speak to you day and night. I love to tell you things, teach you, help you, guide you. I am your Lord and your life. Without Me you can do nothing.

I am speaking to you right now. I am quietly entering your heart and your thoughts right now. You are absorbing My word and My breath of life. You are precious to Me and it is sweet to speak to you this way.

Listen for Me early. When you awaken in the morning, open your eyes and your ears at the same time. As the new day coaxes you awake, allow Me to kiss your thoughts with My words. Allow My voice to embrace your mind with mine.

Listen: Because you are mine, I give you eternal

life, and you shall never lose it or perish throughout the ages—to all eternity you shall never by any means be destroyed. No one can take my love away from you.

Listen: My Father, who has given you to Me, is greater and mightier than all else; and no one is able to snatch you out of His hand. . . .

Listen: The Father and I are One. I am your Good Shepherd. Yours. I am yours. I know you. I love you; you are My own. And it is wonderful, My own, that you know and love Me.

Listen: I want you to hear My voice at all times. I want to be able to speak to you and know you are listening. My heart holds a heavenly kingdom of wisdom, love and of joy to share with you.

If you will listen,
My thoughts will radiate and ignite your own to
a brightness that will light up the whole world.
You will be as a beacon of light on a hill,
fixed and shining
through every storm
and even in the blackest, starless night.

Listen, and I will show you whatever is true, whatever is honorable and worthy of reverence, whatever is just, whatever is pure, whatever is lovely and loveable, whatever is kind and winsome and gracious. I will tell you where virtue and excellence lie, as well as that which is worthy of praise. Think and weigh what I tell you, then fix your mind on these things.

Living in Me, abiding, vitally united to Me is what gives you understanding of majestic qualities. My words remain in you and continue to thrive and bubble up in joy and wisdom in your heart.
If you listen.

And then, dear one,
as My own treasure,
created to bring delight to heaven and the Father
of heaven,
you can ask Me whatever you will
and it shall be done for you.
If you will listen.

John 10:28, 29; Philippians 4:8; 1 Corinthians 6:17;
John 15:7

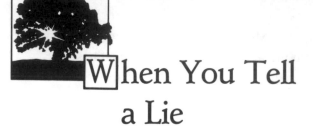

When You Tell a Lie

He feedeth on ashes: a deceived heart hath turned him aside . . .

(Isaiah 44:20a, KJV)

I know when you've been tempted to tell a lie. And I know when you *have* lied. You're afraid the truth won't be good enough. You're afraid the truth won't be acceptable.

I know. I see. I hear.

I want you to know you can come to Me and exchange your lies for my truth. I know the truth, everything there is to know about you, and I never ever reject you.

When you are tempted to lie, I want you to remember I am the only One you need to concern yourself with impressing. If your ways please Me, I'll make even your enemies to be at peace with you. I want you to be impressed with the power of truth.

You may be tempted to lie about your age, your

salary, where you've been, or the people you've dated.

Lies, to Me, are useless and a waste of time. There is no reason for you to lie ever.
The truth spoken is like
a beautiful sunrise over a dirty city,
like a warm blanket on a cold night.
It is My name.

There is life in your speaking the truth; there is only fear in speaking lies. I want you to give yourself permission to speak the truth.

Allow yourself the right
to be exactly who you are and where you are,
to be pleased with who you are
and where you are—
pleased as I am pleased,
not as the world is proud.

Take truth to your heart today. Hold the truth in your thoughts and in the words you speak.

Your true home is in the heart of God. It's where you were born to live and where you are safe. The truth won't hurt you. You can face the consequences of the truth. You can be responsible for the truth.

I am with you.
I will never leave you.
I forgive.

I strengthen.

I love you.

John 14:18; Proverbs 16:7; 12:22; Hebrews 6:18; John 14:6; Deuteronomy 32:4; Colossians 3:9; Ephesians 2:4

When You Are in Need of Protection

The name of the Lord is a strong tower; the
[consistently] righteous man . . . runs into
it and is safe, high [above evil] and strong.
(Prov. 18:10, Amp. Bible)

You feel unsafe, unsure.

You don't like to be alone.

You're frightened, and fear limits the joy you experience in your life. You're trapped in an adventureless existence. What are you afraid of? Pain? Rejection? Are you afraid of making a mistake? Of getting hurt? Of being robbed or killed? Of getting a disease?

Tell me your feelings. I want you to know My feelings, too.

Did you know I am never afraid, worried, frenzied or never driven with terror? Did you know that your

Lord is at peace *always*? Did you know My Spirit—the same as is in Me—lives in you?

I have built a wall of protection around you so that the invisible dragons of the night will not harm you. I have saved you from the terrors of the night. I never sleep, and I am always watching over you.

I save you from the troubles and dangers of the daytime. I am for you. Who can be against you?

But you worry.

You worry because of past experiences when you were hurt. You are afraid to be hurt again. You are afraid I won't keep my word. You are afraid I don't care about you. But I do care. Every hair on your head is numbered.

See Me as your strong tower. See your Lord and Savior as having all glory and majesty, dominion and power both now and forever.

See Me surrounding you and keeping you from evil. See Me bringing you up out of a horrible pit, lifting you gently out of the miry clay of fear and worry. See yourself completely safe, with your feet upon a rock, established in the ways of God.

You will never be happy until you fully sense My loving protection over you.

Jude 24, 25; 2 Thessalonians 3:3; Psalm 40:2

When You Think You Have No Discipline

*If we live by the (Holy) Spirit, let us also walk by
the Spirit. . . . let us go forward walking in line,
our conduct controlled by the Spirit.*
                    (Gal. 5:25, Amp. Bible)

You complain about not having enough time to do
what you think you must do. But the truth is this:
You have been afraid
    of responsibility,
        of saying no to yourself.
            Afraid of lack,
                pain,
                    being left out,
                        going without,
                            being laughed at,
                            failure.
You make *excuses* for not accomplishing what you

think you must accomplish. You have wonderful and exciting ideas, but they stay just that—ideas.
You tell yourself you need
a heavenly boost,
a divine nudge in the ribs,
motivation,
encouragement.
You have need of work that interests and delights you; you have need of peaceful surroundings and a quiet place to pray and spend time with Me daily. Even more than these, you have need of My Spirit.

When you think you have no discipline, you need the attentive care of the Holy Spirit. You need My Spirit to rule in all areas of your life. I listen to your call for help. I am here now to heal and discipline your unruly, fearful heart.
Fill yourself with Me.
The Spirit of Truth is always in you to help
in the way of discipline.
It is not too difficult for you
to learn.
Live in Me.

Ezekiel 36:27; James 1:6; Psalm 143:10; Matthew 7:7; Galatians 5:24

Your Life of
Discipline

Therefore [there is] now no condemnation—no adjudging guilty of wrong—for those who are in Christ Jesus, who live not after the dictates of the flesh, but after the dictates of the Spirit.

(Rom. 8:1, Amp. Bible)

When you feel complete in Me, you will no longer be afraid to be disciplined. You will no longer feel that discipline is condemnation, and a divine punishment. You will feel fulfilled.

You have thoughts in your mind that are not of Me. You can recognize them by their hard, demanding and condemning tone. I did not come to condemn the world, but to save it. Will you allow Me to save you from your mistaken thoughts? You can be as disciplined as you want to be.

When you walk after the flesh you are hard on yourself. You tell yourself you're not doing well enough, or being good enough. You do not take time

to allow Me to be the fulfillment of all your needs.
Do not give place to the devil,

> who is always trying to render you

>> weak and helpless.

You have the very same Spirit of God and Glory in you that lifted Me from the grip of death. You have My mind and you have My blessing.

Deny yourself the luxury of defeat. Take up your cross and follow Me. Discipline does not mean suffering helplessly at My hand; it means to share My Glory.

You will accomplish all that you need to accomplish when I am given the right to guide, help and strengthen you.

I want to be Lord of your life.

John 3:18; Romans 8:5; 1 Peter 5:8; Romans 8:11; Matthew 6:24; John 15:8

When It's Difficult to Trust

The Lord thy God in the midst of thee is mighty; he will save, he will rejoice over thee with joy; he will rest in his love, he will joy over thee with singing.
(Zeph. 3:17, KJV)

I am a giving God. I am neither cruel nor vindictive, as is common with man. Do not think of Me as a human being with human failings.

You can trust Me because I am not limited by your feelings, your ideas, your thoughts. I am bigger than these. I am bigger than any person's interpretation of me.

I always prevail. People may lose, nations may lose, even churches may lose, but I never lose.

I will not lose *you.*

Hold fast to Me as I hold fast to you. Trust Me.

Understand that even when you find it difficult to trust, I am with you.

Be as a little child, and trust.

Isaiah 55:8–9; John 10:27–28

The Everlasting Arms

The Eternal God is your refuge and dwelling place, and underneath are the everlasting arms.
(Deut. 33:27, Amp. Bible)

No matter where you are and no matter what is going on around you, you are safe in Me. I am your refuge and dwelling place. My arms never tire of holding you.

During the day, remember the everlasting arms of God are holding you. Resting in your awareness of Me will bring you closer to trust. Do not strive. I am a God of peace.

Trust Me and enlarge the walls of your understanding. Your soul will expand in quietness. Your entire being will radiate. This is My will for you.

Your dwelling place and your home is in my arms. You can trust that the concerns of your heart are held securely in the promises I have given you. My will for you is that you trust, lean on and confidently hope in

Me. I have said my children are like Mount Zion which cannot be moved, abiding and standing fast forever. As the mountains are round about Jerusalem, so am I round about My people forever.

Don't reject My embrace.

Psalm 125:1, 2

The Overcomer

To him who overcomes (is victorious) I will
grant to eat [of the fruit] of the tree of life,
which is in the paradise of God.
(Rev. 2:7, Amp. Bible)

I know your affliction, distress and pressing trouble—and I am with you. I want you to understand I am your shelter and your strong tower to feel safe in, no matter what your circumstances.

Satan knows the way to your heart is through circumstances. He knows it's easy to discourage you when your body is in pain and when you face a trial. So let your eye be single,

fixed on Me.

Where your treasure is,

your heart is also.

I live in your heart.

You and I become one as you diligently cling to and trust Me. I have said in my written Word that the one who overcomes and conquers Satan's threats, lies and attacks will receive from me hidden manna to eat and a white stone with his or her name written on it.

I give you an eternal identity, as well as a brand new life on earth. Do not be afraid to overcome. Do not be afraid to face the wild storms around you. Do not shrink back from an unruly and disobedient world.

Be of good cheer because I have overcome the world and its sorrows. Because of Me, you overcome. Greed and lust will not defeat you. Temptation will not consume your mind when you overcome evil with good. Choose My goodness and holiness. Choose to be victorious in all that you do and I will give you the fruit from the tree of life.

Affliction is not your master. Trouble and pain are not your guides. I am your Lord and this day I give you power to overcome.

Psalm 61:3; Matthew 6:21; Revelation 2:9, 13, 17

In Times of Temptation

[Better is] he that ruleth his spirit than he
that taketh a city.
(Prov. 16:32, KJV)

You are never alone in your distress. I am with you even in your tumult of self-doubt and temptation. You are tempted in your weakness, not in your strength. But My strength will carry you through on wings of victory. I give you My strength.

Believe I have something better for you. My grace is sufficient. There is victory for every temptation. There is victory *now*.

You will not fall if you dare to believe I have better rewards for you than the goals you pursue outside My will.

Let me strengthen you. Let me help you to see yourself doing My will—victorious. I strengthen you with the right hand of My righteousness. You can be as victorious as you choose to be. And I will guide you away from the path that leads to destruction.

Satan is experienced at presenting evil as good. He is capable of making you believe ugly is beautiful. He is capable of convincing you that self-indulgence is good for you. I will not let you fall if you turn to Me and refuse to be harassed by false appearances of goodness.

I give you the power to see beyond the temptation. I give you wisdom. I give you a heavenly appetite. I give you strength to resist evil. See with holy eyes beyond that which tempts you.

I am there.

1 Corinthians 10:13; Hebrews 2:17, 18

Ending Your War with Yourself

And, beloved, if our consciences (our hearts) do not accuse us—if they do not make us feel guilty and condemn us—we have confidence (complete assurance and boldness) before God.

(1 John 3:21, Amp. Bible)

How often I've called you in love and in tenderness. How often I've sung over you in the night and rejoiced over you in the day. And yet, how often I've heard you curse yourself. How often I've heard your private battle cry against yourself!

Why? Have I waged war against My beloved? Have I instructed you to hurl rebukes and angry insults at My chosen? Am I to wear the uniform of the enemy and take sides against My own?

Never!

I am He who calls you to the glorious kingdom of peace and righteousness.

I am the One who gives you new life,

who yanks sin and hatred from you.
Would you accuse Me of sending you
    that which I have freed you from?
When you came, holding your heart out to Me,
    I lifted you up into My own heart.
I see you as a rare and precious gem
        fitting perfectly in the Father's resplendent
        heavenly crown.
I am making a gem out of you.
I am creating a new heart in you.
    And now you war against that very heart. You
devalue the jewel of God.
Peace I give you my dear one. Peace to be yourself,
    and to enjoy being yourself.
To speak kindly of yourself is to humble yourself.
To hold yourself in esteem is to humble yourself.
To be gentle with yourself is to hold Me in esteem.
Because you love Me,
    end the war with yourself.

Romans 8:1, 31–39

Seeing Yourself Through the Eyes of God

He who gains Wisdom loves his own life; he
who keeps understanding shall prosper and
find good.
(Prov. 19:8, Amp. Bible)

Speak of yourself as though it was I, the Father, describing you. The new life I have given you does not make room for self-hate, self-derision or self-inflicted insults.

You are My own handiwork, My workmanship, recreated in Christ Jesus, born anew that you may do those good works for which I predestined you, taking paths which I prepared ahead of time that you should walk in them—living the good life which I prearranged and made ready for you to live.

Do not be rash to utter harsh words
against yourself.

Be careful with your mouth
and stop your heart
before it is hasty to utter
negative, demeaning words before
God.
I love you!
I call you with an everlasting love
constantly
constantly.
If you were to think of yourself as I think of you,
how different you would be.

Ecclesiastes 5:2; Ephesians 2:10; Jeremiah 31:3

God's Plans for You

*"For I know the plans I have for you," declares
the Lord, "plans to prosper you and not to harm
you, plans to give you hope and a future".*
(Jer. 29:11, NIV)

If you were to think of yourself as I think of you,
how glad, how healthy, how satisfied you would be.
Your mind and body would be at peace. You would
feel an absence of stress, a release from anxiety.

I am already alive in your heart where you have
invited me. I want to fill your heart. I want my word
to flood and be the dominating force in your life. Keep
your heart with all diligence, for out of it flow the very
issues of life.

Why would you war against your own precious
heart? Self-disgust is lifeless and loveless. When you
allow thoughts of hopelessness, it is like jumping into
a deep, empty grave. In the grave there is no life, no
love.

But I am risen from the grave.
  I call you from outside the grave.
    Come out now!
  Leave your war behind.
Bury hopelessness
  but do not bury yourself.
  Sit with Me in heavenly places where I have made
a place for you. You can hear Me better when you are
at my side.
I, your heavenly Father, am ready to pardon,
  gracious and merciful
    slow to anger,
      and full of great, steadfast love.
Shake yourself from the dust,
  loose yourself from the bonds around your neck
and enjoy being a child of My heart.

Proverbs 4:23; Nehemiah 9:17; Ephesians 2:6;
Colossians 3:1

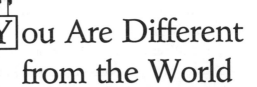

You Are Different from the World

What is born of [from] the flesh is flesh—of
the physical is physical; and what is born of
the Spirit is spirit.
(John 3:6, Amp. Bible)

I regenerate you by My Holy Spirit. When you are
in union with Me, My Spirit molds you into My image
in order that you may share inwardly My likeness.
Do not live the life of the flesh
    any longer.
You now live the life of My Spirit
    if the Holy Spirit of God [really] dwells within
    you—directs and controls you.
You are different now because
though you were born of the flesh once,
    you were born of the Spirit
        when you opened your heart to Me.
    Now you're born again because you're born of the
Spirit. Discover the life of the Spirit. Others may not

41

understand that you are a new person. As a result of your new birth, others may stop caring about you. The world will not celebrate your new nature in Me.

I am now your Lord and Messiah;
you are My child,
and a citizen of the kingdom of God.

You are now no longer an outsider or an alien to the kingdom of God. You are not excluded from the rights of heavenly citizenship. You are different from the world. You now share citizenship with the saints— My own people, consecrated and set apart. You belong to the household of God.
The world around you may complain,
groan,
fight,
destroy,
malign and hurt,
serving Satan's purposes,
but *you* are different.

You are not of the world. You are no longer bound by its limits. You are no longer a slave to pleasure-seeking.

Rejoice that you are different.

Rejoice that you are a partaker of My divine nature.

Rejoice that you are Mine.

Romans 8:9, 29; Galatians 6:15; Ephesians 2:19

The Power You Didn't Know You Had

Now unto him that is able to do exceeding
abundantly above all that we ask or think,
according to the power that worketh in us.
(Eph. 3:20, KJV)

You need to repent of a fretful, fearful heart.
You worry so over problems. You lose sleep.
Your eating habits are poor. Your body hurts.
You ask your friends, "What am I going to do?"
You ask people to pray for you.
You write letters to Christian TV personalities.
And then,
   you come to Me—
      after you hang up the phone—
and say, "Oh, Lord, let your will be done."
   I am not pleased with your anxious thoughts.
   There are times when you choose to become

swallowed up in the old attitude of weakness and failure. You see yourself as inept, incapable and helpless in the face of problems. But why?

I told my disciples, and I tell you, that I give you the power to tread on serpents and scorpions. I have told my disciples, and I tell you, that nothing shall by any means hurt you (Luke 10:19).

Here is the problem: you concentrate, meditate and dwell on weakness, failure and doom, even as you ask that My will be done! My will is that you walk in newness of life. My will is that you see yourself a capable person and that you see Me as the strength of your life. You were created to produce fruit in the heavenly kingdom and to glorify God. You are a Christian, yet you fill your mind with ungodly fears.

You ask of Me, but you give little. Will a man rob God? You cling to your fears. You cling to your time. You cling to your possessions and your income as though these are all there is. Only what you give to others is yours. What pleases me is a happy heart. Your true gifts are those that flow from a happy heart.

Do not tremble at the threats of Satan. I watched him topple downward as he fell out of heaven. The Holy Spirit gives you power to live confidently in the face of danger. I have commanded you in my word to be strong in the power of my might because

in your weakness I am strong.

Lift up the hands

hanging limply at your side.
Strengthen the knees
     that tremble at the threat of danger and trouble.
Put on the full armor of God
     so that the serpents of fear and worry
          can't reach you.

     Realize I am all you need! I have given you power
and love and a sound mind, not a spirit of fear.
Become a friend of obedience. Learn to enjoy obeying
My will.

     My will is that you know who I am, that you love
Me, and that you grasp this truth: You are more than a
conqueror through Me. I give power to the faint and to
those without might I increase strength.

     Show Me.

Isaiah 40:29; Phil. 4:13

The Servant's Goal

Seek ye [first] the kingdom of God; and all
these things shall be added unto you.
(Luke 12:31, KJV)

I take pleasure in My obedient servants who are
not afraid of hard work and who complete tasks
joyfully. I rejoice at all that is accomplished for the
heavenly kingdom. I delight in the fulfillment of My
will.

There awaits a mighty harvest of souls for the
kingdom of God. But there are few laborers to bring in
those who are hurting, lost and wounded. There is
room before the throne of the Father for each hungry
soul. Will you help those who cannot find the way to
Me? Will you go in My name? Will you become a
welcomer in the name of your Lord Jesus Christ,
giving all your energies and drives to God?

If you go on striving to achieve, to prove yourself,
or to make your life "count for something other than

just taking up space" (I've heard you say those words), I must tell you, you will never feel you have achieved enough. You will never satisfy your craving for rewards.

But, oh, dear one!—in Me, your talents and gifts explode with limitless energy and creativity. There is great reward in serving Me as one of My cherished servants. I give the rewards.

Your drive to achieve can be replaced by fresh anointing in My Holy Spirit. Divine zeal replaces an ungodly craving for attention and praise.

You are a hard worker and that is good. It brings pleasure to My heart to see you enjoy your work. I have given you your talents in order that you may multiply them and give them to Me as gifts.

Will you be a gift to Me today?

Romans 12:1; Galatians 2:20

Raising Your Standard of Living

That Christ may dwell in your hearts by faith;
that ye, being rooted and grounded in love. . . .
(Eph. 3:17, KJV)

I am giving you a far higher standard of living than you are accustomed to. I lift you up to an elevated position in My kingdom. You need not grovel in the mud of worldly cares and pursuits.

See My divine example: "Be ye holy; for I am holy."

Accept and understand: "Be ye therefore perfect as My Father which is in heaven is perfect."

This higher walk requires more of you than does a lovely human character. It demands a reflection of My own divine character. Without My character you cannot comprehend how to "love one another, as I have loved you."

To understand and experience this higher standard of life, you must learn to become easily molded and

48

shaped by My Word. The happiness you experience in being shaped by Me is exquisite, holy and sublime, for in My presence is fullness of joy.

The Christian is to be transformed and shaped into My very image. You become more like Me every day.

This unfolding higher standard reveals to you a deeper inner life by My Spirit. It is a life that reaches your thoughts, motives, desires and requires you to love Me with all your heart, soul, mind, and strength. Your heart must become single in purpose, so outwardly and inwardly your life will take on new vibrancy as you reflect the personality of the Beloved.

You will no longer accept impurity or unholy thoughts and feelings, because the presence of your beloved Savior is more real to you than anything in the material world. Every day becomes holy, every footstep is dedicated to the Lord. Your desire becomes to live to the glory of God, pleasing Him only.

Your standard of living and Mine are one.

1 John 3:2; 1 Peter 1:14–16

Learning to Be Satisfied

And my people shall be satisfied with my
goodness, saith the Lord.
                                    (Jer. 31:14, KJV)

You have looked for satisfaction in other places,
but I satisfy you. You have given yourself to
endeavors, projects, labors and relationships, but
never experienced the feeling of satisfaction you crave
and deserve.

The child of God *deserves* the feeling of satisfaction.
The child of God deserves to know and be familiar
with My words, "Well done, good and faithful
servant." You are My child, and you deserve to feel
content and satisfied in whatsoever state you find
yourself.

I gave My life so that satisfaction could be yours. I
conquered dissatisfaction and discontent. I have begun
a work in you which I promise to complete.

I give you a new sense of purpose *now*.

Be confident that I am with you.

Take My hand in yours and hold fast.
I am faithful and I establish you
and I keep you from evil that keeps you
dissatisfied.
The secret of living a satisfied life is to know My love,
which passes human knowledge.
In Me you are perfectly
accepted and cherished.
I love, forgive, strengthen and renew you.

To know My love is to know the mercy of God.

It is My joy to give you My satisfaction.
Today hear My loving words to you.

In Me you are complete.

See yourself as having died with Me to the hunger
for material things. You have escaped from the world's
crude desires to own everything that pleases and
attracts your eye.

Do not live as if you still belong to the world.
Know how much I enjoy your love; enjoy My
goodness and My love toward you and be satisfied.

Ephesians 3:19; Colossians 2:20

Your Personal Fragrance

*"I will refresh Israel like the dew from
heaven; she will blossom as the lily and root
deeply in the soil like cedars in Lebanon.
Her branches will spread out, as beautiful
as olive trees, fragrant as the forests of
Lebanon."*

(Hosea 14:5, 6, TLB)

The happy heart is a sweet fragrance to Me. Your
heart must be trained, however, to be happy. You train
your unruly heart in the skills of happiness.
I give you My Spirit to help you,
 to form a beautiful pattern for your life,
  to create a beautiful aroma
   with your thoughts and attitudes
    for My own delight.
The sense of smell is the most fragile and delicate
of your senses. You recoil from foul smells that cling to
the body and pollute the air, but you are blessed when

the glorious fragrance of My perfume permeates all.

    This fragrance describes you! Your happy heart is more beautiful than the sweetness of the olive tree. Your love for Me is like a heavenly fragrance, not only reaching

    Me, but touching your world.

        The happy heart is like cedar;

            you become a savory expression of Me,

            the source of life

                and all that is beautiful.

2 Corinthians 2:15

Refreshing like the Dew

Your lips drop sweetness as the honeycomb, my
bride; milk and honey are under your tongue.
(Song of Sol. 4:11, NIV)

My servant Noah built an altar and sacrificed a
burnt offering to Me after the ark landed upon dry
ground. It was a sweet smelling fragrance to Me, and
My heart was moved.

Unselfish gifts given in love are a sweet fragrance
to Me. The unselfish heart is a happy one. For as you
present your unselfish love-gifts, I meet all your needs
according to the riches of My glory.

In My word, which I have given to you as your
treasure, I have told you that our love for one another
is a fragrance permeating the atmosphere. You express
your love through your words, "which drop sweetness
as the honeycomb."

Complaining is not a delight to Me. Fault-finding
is not a delight to Me. Ruminating over past hurts is

not a delight to Me. Fretfulness is not a delight to Me. Fear is never a delight to Me, for I am love and love casts out fear.

Allow My Spirit to refresh you like dew from heaven with loving words of faith to water your spirit.

Your personal fragrance is spawned in the attitudes of your heart.

Your fragrance is your message.

Philippians 4:18, 19

God's Thoughts Toward You

For I know the thoughts that I think toward
you, saith the Lord, thoughts of peace, and
not of evil, to give you an expected end.
(Jer. 29:11, KJV)

It is My desire that you know My thoughts toward you
    that your eyes be opened
        and your mind enlightened
            that you may know and understand.
    I want you to know the rich glory of your
inheritance in Me, and My incomparably great power
that is in you. I want your mind renewed by the same
mighty power that raised Me from the dead and seated
Me in the place of honor at God's right hand in
heaven.
The Father holds you snugly
    in His thoughts with love.
        His thoughts and plans for you
           are good

and hold glory beyond your dreams.

Release yourself from the prison of human reasoning. You have been a prisoner of lies. You have believed that you are not worthy of being gloriously blessed. Do not think you were called to live a life of heartache. You have considered yourself an outcast, one whom no one seeks after and for whom no one cares. Even if you have not spoken these thoughts aloud, you have allowed them to be your master.

I will heal your wounds, and release you from these chains of despair into the arms of Love. Choose love and goodness from this day on. No longer accept a life under the oppressor's yoke.

You shall no more be a slave of ungodly lusts and passions and lack of self-respect.

My loving thoughts toward you also break the chains of pride. You need not defend yourself, clawing so frantically, like a cat thrown in water. I am the One who defends you.

I am rich in mercy toward you. It is My will that you open the eyes of your heart and see what an incredible quality of love the Father has given you through Me.

Jeremiah 30:17; Ephesians 1:18–20

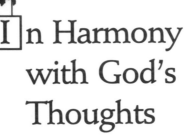

In Harmony with God's Thoughts

See what [an incredible] quality of love the
Father has given (shown, bestowed on) us.
(1 John 3:1, Amp. Bible)

I have loved you just as the Father has loved Me.

My thoughts toward you are filled with My desire for your good. You cannot separate My loving thoughts from you. Neither can tribulation, distress, persecution, famine, nakedness, peril or sword! Your own selfish thoughts will separate you from hearing from Me, but I am still there.

When I look upon you, I do not see a victim of circumstances. I expect you to be victorious. When I look upon you, I do not think, "Oh, what a poor and pathetic thing we have here." I think, "There is My child called by My name to trust Me." I keep you in

perfect peace when your mind is fixed solidly on Me,
unmoveable
and in total harmony
with My thoughts.

When I think of you I see you crowned splendidly
in mercy and I see you wearing that crown with
dignity and trust.

When I think of you I see you submitted to Me
and with the eyes of your soul open to Me.

When I think of you I see a child of God taking Me
at My word.

I see you loving My love.

I see you thankful for My mercy and for the gift of
eternal life I have given you.

I see you loving My Word.

I see you rejoicing that your name is written in the
Lamb's Book of Life.

I see you proud and thrilled to be called by My
name and walking in My spirit.

I see you taking up your cross and following Me
without complaint, in harmony with My thoughts.

John 15:9; Romans 8:35; Isaiah 26:3

When You Don't Think God Is Answering Your Prayers

Then you will call, and the Lord will answer; you
will cry for help, and he will say: Here am I.
(Isa. 58:9, NIV)

You think I am not answering your prayers?
You think I don't hear?

I am not a human being. I do not lie.

There is no need to plead for My answers to your prayers. There is no need to beg for mercy from Me. You already have your answers and you already have My mercy. I freely give to you. I flood your life with good things.

> Surely goodness and mercy
> flood your soul.
> You have the ability,

by My Spirit,
to create a flurry of goodness
and mercy around you
so all who know you can sense
the presence of God.

I am the Giver of Life, the Light of the World. I never hesitate, never wonder. I know My promises, because *I am* the promises I make.

I remind you of My written Word: "If you abide in me, and my words abide in you, you shall ask whatever you will, and it shall be given unto you." "The effective, fervent prayer of the righteous shall avail much."

No word from the Father is without power. He watches over His word with a fiery eye, and He breathes the flame of life into it.

Your faith and trust in Me and the promises I have given you are of great value.

Do not worship answered prayer.

Worship your *Lord* and Savior Jesus Christ.

Numbers 23:19; John 15:7; 8:29

In the Father's Will

Teach me to do Your will, for You are my God.
(Ps. 143:10, Amp. Bible)

Open the eyes of your heart and see your Lord and Savior. You will see that you can do as I did. You can be sure you are in the Father's will. And when you are in His will, you can be certain that your prayers are answered.

Ask what you will.

When you complain your prayers aren't answered soon enough, you are limiting your faith. When you trust Me, you can be absolutely certain even as I am certain of the faithful heart of the Father.

When you trust My judgment, you are absolutely safe in Me. When you trust that I know how and when to answer, you can be at peace, even as I walked in peace trusting the Father.

Many who have gone before you were righteous believers and lived in My will. Many before you waited for answered prayer. And in their waiting, they discovered, as you can, the joy in trusting Me.

Even confined within the walls of a dark, dank and filthy prison with body aching and mind still echoing the swirling insults flung for faith in Me—even then, there is the joy of answered prayer.

Before you call I answer.

I came to do the will of the Father. I came to the world as a man, not to do My own will and live in the limited human realm only, but to do the will of the Father who sent Me. I want you to meditate on My words: "I always do the things that are pleasing to My Father."

It is God's will that you please Him. Your faith pleases Him.

Trust His answers.

John 4:34

When Your Heart Is Broken

Peace I leave with you; My [own] peace I now give and bequeath to you. Not as the world gives do I give to you. Do not let your heart be troubled, neither let it be afraid—stop allowing yourself to be agitated and disturbed; and do not permit yourself to be fearful and intimidated and cowardly and unsettled.

(John 14:27, Amp. Bible)

My heart is large enough to hold your hurt as well as your joy. I am with you in tears and in laughter.

You may be tempted to think that I have afflicted you. But I have not treated you badly and I have not forgotten you. I do not love you less when things go wrong. My love for you is from everlasting to everlasting. My love for you is perfect. Powerful.

I have called you to a higher walk. I have called you to a walk of faith. This walk requires more than

perfect relationships in your life. It requires a living
relationship
    with Me
every minute of every day,
    no matter what the circumstances may be.
    This walk may not be easy. It may not be smooth.
    But I am always at work in you so you will choose
    Me and act according to My purpose.
Let Me comfort your hurting heart.

Philippians 2:13; Matthew 28:20

# New Choices

> *My son, give me your heart, and let your*
> *eyes observe and delight in my ways.*
> (Prov. 23:26, Amp. Bible)

I have covered you with a holy robe of righteousness. You wear the clothing of salvation. (Do you know what that means?)

Right now, today, at this moment, it means you are saved from the agonized cry of despair. I have seen all that has happened in your life. I have seen every person who has walked across your days.

I know.

I see.

I listen.

I *AM*.

Right now, at this moment,
I AM holding you, loving you, comforting you.
My voice is softly singing to you
and it is I who lifts your chin,
urging you to take
the garland of beauty I give you

for the ashes you have been wearing.
Take the perfumed oil of joy
instead of the bleak
and futile stains
of sorrow.
Wear praise
like a golden robe
and the heavy, burdened and failing spirit
will flee from you.

Isaiah 61:3; Philippians 4:4

# Becoming Bold

And Jesus came and spake unto them,
saying, All power is given unto me in
heaven and in earth.
(Matt. 28:18, KJV)

Whose power, or authority, do you trust?
If you trust your own authority,

if you trust your own merits,

if you trust your own abilities,
you have nothing to trust.

Why would you be bold if you have nothing to trust?

In Me only can you be bold. In Me you can have confidence to go forward, never shrinking back, always assured that I am with you. All things have been put under My feet. I am given a name that is above every name.

If you believe it is by Me that all things exist, and if you believe you are called by My name and you are one with me, a member of My body, My flesh and of My bones, then you can have boldness.

Shyness is never a virtue. There is no shy person in heaven. The Spirit of the Lord makes you bold. The Spirit of the Lord gives you confidence. The Spirit builds you up, never tears you down.

Do not confuse humility with timidity. Timidity is not of Me. I am not timid. Boldness is not reserved for a few select people. Allow your heart to be filled and you will sense a new boldness and you will sense timidity leaving you forever.
Today
face yourself and your world with boldness,
being confident whose you are
    and let us enjoy
        flinging aside your fears.

Ephesians 5:30; 1 Timothy 2:5

When You Feel Lonely

"Though the mountains be shaken and the hills be removed, yet my unfailing love for you will not be shaken nor my covenant of peace be removed," says the Lord, who has compassion on you.

(Isa. 54:10, NIV)

You see yourself as a small sparrow alone on a housetop. Your heart quakes. I hear your groaning in the late hours. Your eyes dull; your soul despairs.

But I am with you.

If you are lauded

    as the star of a million parades,

        or if you are alone

            as a frightened bird on a rooftop,

                I am there.

If your name commands the reverence of nations

    and your laurels march before you

        or if you huddle

chilled, friendless and poor against a wall,
                    I am there.
If you sleep in the beds of kings
        and ride the wings of skillful wisdom in all things,
            or if you shiver alone
                    with pain and muddled thoughts,
                    I am there.
If joyful laughter floods your house
        and the smells of bubbling pots of food
            and bulging ovens pour happily from your
        windows
                or if you sit hunched, cross-legged and
                alone
                    spooning dinner from a can,
                    I am there.
If you leap like a deer
        across gymnasium floors,
            muscles taut and body lithe—
                or if you amble slowly, heavily
                    from sitting place to sitting place
                    I am there.
If you love to conquer impossible worlds,
        wielding the powerful sword of the Spirit
            and the mighty banner of faith that I give to
        you,
                or if you cower in fear of failure
                    or rebuke,
                    I am there.

If you awaken each day robust with health
    or if pain envelops every pore
        I am there.
If your friends and loved ones
    press in against you, their affection never waning,
        and if your years are laced in gold
            with precious human love,
                or if you feel abandoned
                    by every soul you ever trusted,
                        I am there.
If you fly the heights and scour the depths;
    If you freely move through clouds
        soaring over the earth with arms outspread,
            or if you fall with clipped wings,
                confined within the prison
                    of a carnal mind,
                        I am there.
If you celebrate the rising of the sun
    and the going down of the same
        and if you greet the dawn
            with trembling expectation,
                I am there.
If your eyes grow dull and your soul despairs
    and your voice is without a song,
        I am there.
I am there in sunlight and in shadows.
    I am there in hunger and in fatness,
        in your youth and in old age.

I am there so you may turn to me.

I stick to you, like your own skin.

The mountains of the earth will shake and crumble,

Yet My tender love for you is never shaken—

not a shiver,

not a breath,

not the barest vibration or change.

Because I am there with you.

Psalm 139:9, 10; Proverbs 18:24

Hidden
Resentment

Let us go right in, to God himself, with
true hearts fully trusting him to receive us,
because we have been sprinkled with
Christ's blood to make us clean, and
because our bodies have been washed with
pure water.

(Heb. 10:22, TLB)

You hide resentment in a forest of other
negative thoughts. You have been hurt, maligned. You
haven't been treated fairly. You've been stolen from,
crushed and cursed, but you shrug with a casual
"holy" look
            and try not to think about it.
You are like one hopping barefoot on the frozen ice
    while insisting your toes are warm.
The hurts rage against you;
    storms of anger assail your peace of mind
    and yet you seek to be a teacher of peace;

74

you eagerly strive for a place in ministry.
Resentment, because it is hidden,
    is tangled in rapidly spreading jealousy,
        vengefulness and a desperate hunger
            to control others.

Talk to me and release your resentment to Me. Tell
Me; trust Me with your secrets. I won't faint if you
become emotional. Your fear of admitting resentment
keeps you from feeling at peace with your world.

You strive. You find fault with others. You are
difficult to get along with. Allow Me to calm your
inner storm. Allow Me to remove resentment and pour
the balm of My Spirit over the sores that have gone so
long unattended.

Then I will give you
    sweetness for your turmoil.
I will give you trust
    for your fearful suspicion.
I will give you an open, vulnerable heart
    for your isolated, walled-in gifts,
        and freedom
            in exchange for chains.

I forgive.
    I renew.
        I revitalize.
            I heal.

TODAY, dare to face those resentful feelings which
will rage within you until the hour you admit and

confess and release them to Me.

This is the hour. Confess your hidden resentments. Take My hand and trust Me as I assure you that no matter what you've been through, nothing can defeat or destroy you. I turn all things to good.

Hebrews 12:15

Hiding from God

Blessed—happy, fortunate [to be envied]—is he
who has forgiveness of his transgression
continually exercised upon him,
whose sin is covered.

(Ps. 32:1, Amp. Bible)

Your chin is stiff when you look away from Me
like that. Your eyes are dull; your countenance is
without sparkle.

Oh, for one quick glance of your precious face
toward Me; *one* gesture in My direction!

You have not forgotten Me; that I know, because
you push so hard against Me. You have a thousand
elbows, all jabbing at the Comforter.

But My love song for you
> doesn't miss a note.

My eye is always upon you.
> You haven't pierced or killed Me.
> I can't be crushed by you.

Where can you go from My Spirit?

Where can you flee from My presence?

If you ascend into My heaven,
                    I am there.
If you make your bed in Sheol, the place of the dead,
                    I am there.
If you take the wings of the morning
        and dwell in the uttermost parts of the sea,
             even there My hand shall lead you,
                 and My right hand shall hold you.
If you say, "Surely the darkness shall cover me,
        and the night shall be the only light about me,"
             even the darkness can hide nothing from Me.
The night shines as the day in the kingdom of God.
The darkness and the night are both alike to Me.
        For I formed you.
        I knit you together in your mother's womb.
Your frame is never hidden from Me.
When you were formed intricately
        and curiously wrought
             as if embroidered with various colors,
                 My eyes saw your unformed substance.
All the days of your life
        were written in My book
             before they took shape.
How precious are My thoughts toward you.
        Don't hide from Me.

Psalm 139:7–18

When You Are in the Valley of Uncertainty

Search me [thoroughly], Oh God, and know
my heart! Try me, and know my thoughts!
And see if there is any wicked or hurtful
way in me, and lead me
in the way everlasting.
(Ps. 139:23, 24, Amp. Bible)

When you are uncertain, it is because you long for the knowledge of Me.

When you are uncertain, your eyes do not behold goodness clearly, and it is difficult to hear the song of joy within you. When you are uncertain, you do not understand what is the good and perfect will of the Father. Then it is time to pause from the cares of life and listen to My Spirit.

Allow Me to search and know your heart. Allow me to try and know your thoughts.

When you give Me the right
to enter your heart,
you give Me permission
to cleanse it.

You grant Me permission to release the vexation of
not knowing, which has held you bound.

Do you remember the Valley of Decision when you
first came to Me? I give you the right to visit the Valley
of Decision again in order to hear new direction and
gain new direction by My Spirit.

Because you are Mine, you will not settle for the
shallow or that which pleases the senses. There is a
way that seems right to a person, and appears to be
straight, but the child of God knows that at the end of
this way is death.

You hunger for My words, "Well done good and
faithful servant." Rejoice and do not be easily swayed.
The child of God who is hasty of spirit exposes and
exalts his folly.

Rule your own spirit.

Understanding is a wellspring of life to you
when you are wise in heart.

Wisdom and understanding grow
as you listen and heed My Word—

leaning, trusting,
and building confidence
in Me.

Proverbs 14:12, 29; Joel 3:14

When You Don't Know What to Say

The mind of the wise instructs his mouth, and
adds learning and persuasiveness to his lips.
(Prov. 16:23, Amp. Bible)

Do not be intimidated by human wisdom.

Do not hold back because you feel your words will
not be impressive.

I use the simple things of life and cause them to be
powerful.

I have chosen babes to influence kings.

I create a new vocabulary in your mouth.

I create a new mouth in you.

I have created a new communication in you.

Where you once belched words like smoke
and meaningless vapors,
you now build cities of gold
with words of life.

No longer drip empty phrases
    that dry up in the sun,
        but speak words as apples of gold.
Rule your spirit
    and speak words of discretion and wisdom,
        deep as water,
            plenteous and fathomless.

Your words are fed by My fountain of skillful, godly wisdom and are as a gushing stream—sparkling, fresh, pure and life-giving.

I give you the ability to bring your heavenly Father much delight by the glistening expressions of His own mind. So allow the truth I have taught you to permeate your words. My heart will be glad and will rejoice when your lips speak the words I have taught you, when your lips pour forth the fountain of life in your heart.

Today, allow Me to give you the tongue of a disciple, the tongue of one who is taught by Me in order that you always know how to speak a word in season to him who is weary—including yourself.

I waken you morning by morning.

I awaken your ear to hear My words.

Proverbs 16:24; 18:4; Isaiah 50:4

When You Want to Gain Respect

So shall you find favor, good understanding
and high esteem in the sight [or judgment]
of God and man.
(Prov. 3:4, Amp. Bible)

You want to gain respect of people, and there
is only one way to be held in high esteem: to be
esteemed by Me. When you want to gain respect,
meditate on pleasing Me.

You please Me by binding the truth around your
neck, and writing mercy and kindness upon the tablet
of your heart. You shall find favor and good
understanding of God and your fellowman by leaning
on, trusting, and gaining perfect confidence in Me.

When you rely on your own insight and understanding, you lose footing in the ranks of heaven's
generals. But a good person obtains favor of the Lord.
And when you choose an uncompromisingly righteous
walk, you have the full attention of God,

who causes you to flourish like a tree
     planted by streams of living water,
          bringing forth fruit in its season.
Everything you do shall prosper
     and your leaf shall not fade or whither.
     You have My sweet, satisfying companionship.
With your foot on an even place, you will walk in your
integrity and please Me.
     When your ways please Me, you have respect.

Proverbs 12:2; Psalm 1:3; 25:14.

The Joyful Person

Go your way, eat the fat, drink the sweet,
and send portions to him for whom nothing
is prepared; for this day is holy to our Lord;
and be not grieved and depressed, for the
joy of the Lord is your strength and
stronghold.
(Neh. 8:10, Amp. Bible)

I love you because you have chosen
    to live in My heart,
which knows no ugliness
    and no sin.
I love you because you are Mine;
    I can speak to you
    and you hear Me.
    When you lack joy it is because you seek the
experience of joy above Me. When you ache and long
for just one taste of joy and feel it not, it is because
you look for it in places outside your heart.

I can tell you to rejoice because I AM joy. To rejoice is to drink of the essential essence of God, to be in My presence.

You say, "But, Lord, You are invisible. How can I be joyful when I can't see You?"

You are being garrisoned at this moment by My power through your faith. Is this not enough to make you exceedingly glad?

Even though you may be distressed by trials for a little while, and suffer temptation, the genuineness of your faith becomes tested and it is more precious than perishable gold. Gold is always refined and purified by fire.

And you, without having seen Me, love Me. That which you cannot see brings you the greatest pleasure in all life. I constantly give, because I want your joy and gladness to be full, complete and overflowing.

It is a delight for Me to tell you of the wonders in store for you when you live vitally united to Me, when My words remain in your thoughts as permanent fixtures.

You have ached for eternal joy and settled for drips of fun. How can you laugh with My holy laugh when Satan's talons are pulling you down into a sea of complaints?

You know the Source of joy;
  now taste and see that
    I am good.

1 Peter 1:5–7; John 15:11.

Getting to the Place of Joy

You will show me the path of life; in Your
presence is fullness of joy, at Your right
hand there are pleasures for evermore.
(Ps. 16:11, Amp. Bible)

I was delivered up according to the definite
and fixed purpose and settled plan of God for your
sake. The Father raised me up, liberating Me from the
pangs of hell; it was not possible for Me to be
controlled or retained by Death. The Father raised Me
to life and exalted Me at His right hand.

There, I received from the Father the promised
Holy Spirit, and I have poured Him out upon you. The
joy of the presence of God is the fruit of the Holy
Spirit, who is yours.

Whoever calls upon the name of the Lord will be
saved. And you, dear friend, I save from joylessness.
By My Spirit, take gladness, delight and awe at all
things beautiful. There are no imitations for joy.

Miracles fade. Signs and wonders may change from generation to generation. All ambition and spiritual competition falls to dust. But the fruit of the spirit can only be known by My Spirit, whom you have.

See Me now and let joy encircle your head like a garland. Let it seep into every thought, every dream, every desire.

There is a river and you must know it. The streams of this river rush forth and make the city of God glad, for the Father himself is in the midst of her.

I promise you that your faith in Me will give you rivers of living water flowing out of your innermost being.

Joy makes you intensely aware of every living thing, everything that your eye sees.

Your senses are sharpened,
        and you are lifted beyond mere living
            into a realm of ecstasy
    that no godless soul can comprehend.
Take your exaltation of spirit.
    Take your gladness.
    Take your delight and awe at all things
    beautiful.
TODAY, come into My presence and share My joy.

Psalm 16:11; 46:4, 5; John 7:38; Acts 2:21–35.

Discovering the Small Joys of Life

Then was our mouth filled with laughter,
and our tongue was singing. Then they
said among the nations, The Lord has done
great things for them. The Lord has done
great things for us! We are glad!
(Ps. 126:2, 3, Amp. Bible)

I have done great things for you. I have set you free from the captivity of sorrow. I have set you free from being captive to emotions.

You place your life on so great a slab of grandiose demands. Where is the still *small* voice of gladness?

You sowed in tears and now you shall reap in joy and singing. Be receptive to the often small voice of joyfulness around you. Do not neglect the little, often unnoticed moments of pleasure. Do not sacrifice the enchantment of a quiet morning for the explosive celebration of noontime.

All moments are meteoric,
   filled with delight,
      stories and mysteries.
         I give you the mind of a hunter,
            the heart of a poet,
               the energy of an athlete
            to discover new joys daily.
               I give you
               the choreography of the rain,
and the skilled performance
   of the winter's first snowfall.
         Have you found a song in a brother's face?
            Have you touched the velvet crest of dawn
               in the simple clasp
                  of a loved one's hand?
   To know Me is to experience a sharpening of all
your senses. You become the artist and the statesman.
You become the teacher and the student. You can
become all you were created to be.
   Tell Me your discoveries.
   Tell me what delights you.

1 Timothy 6:17

The Joys of Discovery

Therefore with joy will you draw water
from the wells of salvation.
(Isa. 12:3, Amp. Bible)

Your sense of discovery, of unquenchable
curiosity and delight is good to behold. Others will be
drawn to you by My Spirit because of your compelling,
holy enthusiasm for discovering even the tiniest delights of My kingdom.

There are no tears in any corner of heaven because
there is no end to the joy of discovery. Joy feeds and
creates itself like love.

Tears will no longer encrust your cheeks, My dear
friend, because you know and trust Me.

And you have learned the joy of discovery.

I give you a holy microscope
to learn of the subtlest thrills of life
    in My Spirit—
even those which are hard to bear:

>   sickness,
>   pain,
>   loss,
>   war.

Use your holy microscope
        and discover
My Spirit is unquenchable.

You have My mind to create delight, no matter
what the circumstances you are in. Have you ever
examined a plant cell? Ever given names to the
inhabitants of the bottom of the ocean floor? Ever
counted the teeth of a whale? Gazed into the eye of a
parrot? Have the feathers of the ostrich swept across
your brow? Have you heard the angels singing in the
night? Have you clapped your hands with trees that
always praise their Maker? Do you hear the rocks cry
out? Can you hear the snore of a beetle?

How developed is your sense of discovery?

Psalm 8:3; 19:1

When You Lack Energy

It is the Spirit that gives life—He is the Life-giver; the flesh conveys no benefit whatever—there is no profit in it. The words [truths] that I have been speaking to you are spirit and life.
(John 6:63, Amp. Bible)

Life and energy are found in Me.

Do not seek life among the dead. Dead works will wear you down, will rob you of energy. Dead works are those activities that are not brought to life by My Spirit.

Where the Spirit of the Lord is there is liberty. There is life. Fear will weary you and exhaust your mind and body. Why waste away when I renew your heart day after day?

Joy is the mother of enthusiasm. When you lack energy, you have lost your joyous gift to

truly see

truly feel

truly love.

Delighting in Me
is the source of your energy.
Joy is the exuberance
that cannot be quenched by prison,
beatings,
hunger,
or any of Satan's tools
designed to make your heart weary.

My child, Satan has been a liar from the beginning, and He seeks to steal your goods, your health, your relationships, your ministry, your leisure, your productivity, your time, because he wants your joy.

Resist the urge to listen to his lies. Satan will flee from you if you force and submerge your thoughts in Me.

Sin robs you of energy. I came to the world to save sinners.

Pride robs you of energy. Pride marches before destruction, and a haughty attitude precedes a fall.

Your heart will fail
as a result of iniquity.
Your bones will wax old
through your roaring all the day long.
Sin is a heavy burden,
too heavy for you.
But I am calling you
to take My yoke upon you

and learn of Me.
I am gentle (meek) and humble in heart.
I will give you rest, and refreshment
    because My yoke is good.
My burden is light and easy to be borne
    because I love you.
I will forgive and restore to you
    all that has been lost and destroyed.
Take My energy.
    It is your spiritual treasure.
        It is your rightful inheritance.
    Arise, shine, for your light has come, and the glory
of the Lord rises upon you—the Lord rises upon you
and His glory appears over you! You will look and be
radiant; your heart will throb and swell with joy.
    I am your everlasting light and your glory. Your
days of sorrow are ended if you will allow Me to prove
I can be your energy.

2 Corinthians 4:16, 17; 1 Timothy 1:15; Proverbs 16:18;
Psalm 40:12; 32:3; 38:4; Matthew 11:28–30; Isaiah 60:1,
2b, 5a, 19.

When You Want Recognition

All nations will come to your light; mighty
kings will come to see the glory of the Lord
upon you.

(Isa. 60:3, TLB)

Why do you desire recognition? Have you accomplished something wonderful for Me?

Do you long to see your Lord exalted and lifted up through your doing? Is that why you labor and toil in My ministry? Or do you feel a holy drive to bring Me glory and praise?

Do you not know that you are already recognized, honored and highly esteemed by Me? I am more influential than presidents and kings, bigger than family, employers, teachers and the multitudes of nations. By Me all matter is held together. By Me the stars suspend in the heavens. By Me the worlds were created. By Me a new nature and a new person was created in you.

You will receive recognition in the world, but for different reasons. The world recognizes you for what you *do*. You are recognized by Me for who you *are*. You carry the banner of God: you walk in My Spirit. You shall not go unrecognized.

The glory the Father gave Me
> I give to you
> > in order that you will be one
> > > with the rest of My dear children
> > > who are called by My name

and walk in My Spirit—
> one, as the Father and I are one!

There is no higher reward in this life than the knowledge of My approval and recognition. When you feel you need recognition, come to Me first, not the world and not My body of believers. I'll give you more than you ask. I'll give you My *glory*.

How will you receive the glory I give you?

You will call upon Me and ask My help. You will call upon Me and give Me back what I have given to you. You may keep what is yours, but give the glory to Me.

Colossians 1:16–18; John 17:22.

When You Need Relief

Return to your rest, O my soul, for the
Lord has dealt bountifully with you.
(Ps. 116:7, Amp. Bible)

You cry in need of rest. You crave a diversion. And I want to ease your furrowed brow. I want to wrap the arms of My Spirit around you and give you rest.

I have delivered your life from death, your eyes from tears, and your feet from stumbling and falling. When you are in need of relief, come to Me in Spirit and in truth and you will find it.

But if you turn to carnal devices for relief, you will yet be in need of relief.

Pleasure won't relieve you. Sleep won't relieve you. Worldly devices won't relieve you.

My Spirit does not merely dull your pain or satisfy your desire for relief.

I replenish,

restore,

    invigorate,

       renew

         and breathe a fresh wave

      of heavenly contentment within you.

I have promised to give you more than you ask or dream of.

Are you in need of a new vision?

Do you desire a sweeter relationship with those close to you?

Do you long for friends to share your heart with?

Are you wanting a change of circumstances?

Are you in need of deliverance?

To find relief, enter into My rest. Enter into My heart. Enter into prayer. Begin by quieting your heart and withdrawing peacefully in the stillness of the hour where you will be undisturbed by outside influences. Refrain from boisterously assaulting the air with battle cries as you approach the throne of grace. Be still and calmly concentrate on the presence of the Father.

Allow yourself to leave the cares of the world, your daily routine, and every concern outside yourself. Do not rush. Breathe deeply, slowly. Release your attachment to the cares around you. Let go of the control of your life.

Adore, trust and love your heavenly Father in My name.

Adore and worship.

Adore and magnify.

As you praise your King and Savior, sense yourself engulfed in the endless ocean of our love for you. Give the Holy Spirit complete control of your praise, and as you continue to worship do not concern yourself with the words you speak. Simply allow yourself to freely communicate, adore, trust, love and worship.

Yield and allow the Holy Spirit to fill and help you in your weakness. You will feel release as you soar into the blissful presence of the Father God. The Holy Spirit will express himself through you; and God, who knows all things and all the thoughts of your heart, hears and understands.

Allow your expression of love to flow freely. You were created to share in this exquisite life of the Father. Expand your worship, praise and adoration of Him in order to give Him more of you.

This is your fountain of life; worship is your relief. Such holy and perfect relief is God himself.

Psalm 116:8; Romans 8:26–27

When You Feel the Chains of Guilt Around You

I have blotted out as a thick cloud your
trangressions, and as a cloud your sins.
Return to Me, for I have redeemed you.
(Isa. 44:22, Amp. Bible)

Confess your sins so I can forgive you, relieving you of the painful burden of sin and failure.

You tend to see yourself as unclean, as far removed from all that is heavenly. I see you as My precious child.

You tend to see yourself as a hopeless backslider, a poor refugee. I see you as Mine.

You can never dig too deep a hole for Me to pull you out. You can never take on Satan's desperate lifestyle so fully that I cannot find you.

Who is your accuser? Who is the one who condemns? Do not think of your Lord as a man, quick to anger, vengeful and spiteful.

You have grumbled that My ways are too hard, too prickly and too demanding. These words you did not learn from Me. Your thoughts have not absorbed My thoughts.

Examine the words you speak, because it is you who are hardest on yourself.

If you take the chains of sin upon yourself and expect integrity and fair dealings from the Prince of Evil, you are deceived. You walk into a pit blindfolded because you dreamed of roses there. You shriek with broken bones and shake your fist at heaven, claiming God has dealt unfairly with you.

Oh, afflicted one, storm-tossed and not comforted, I want to give you jewels for your foundation.

When the wicked forsakes his way and the unrighteous person his thoughts, and when he returns to Me, I will have love, pity and mercy for that one. The Father abundantly pardons and He loves to multiply blessings.

You shall establish yourself in righteousness, in conformity with the Father's will and order. Hear Me in the wrestling of your mind, for My call of love is true and powerful.

I shall put you in a place far from the thought of oppression or destruction. I shall lift you up above guilt and shame, and sin shall no longer be your master. I shall lift you up from fear and from terror, for it shall not come near you.

Do not caress guilt as though you deserve it. Confess to Me your wanderings, and the ease with which you curse the One who loves you. Guilt is not your friend, and feelings of guilt do not make you holy or clean. *Be holy as I am.*

It is not too great a sacrifice to yield all your guilt to Me. In return I'll give you a new and cleansed heart. You have condemned yourself by imagining there are sins I cannot forgive. Give up that thought. Sacrifice and yield your thoughts to Me.

Allow Me to purify and cleanse your heart by My own blood, which pours in a constant healing and forgiving flow to wash away all thoughts and acts contrary to the will of My Father.
I give you the garments of praise so you can throw away
     that old tattered and
        foul-smelling coat of
           collected sins and guilt.

When you are forgiven, you are free. Whom the Son makes free is free indeed.

Isaiah 55:7, 8, 9; 54:11, 14

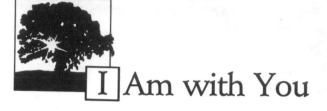

I Am with You

"I will never leave you nor forsake you."
(Heb. 13:5, NKJV)

There is nothing to fear if you will concentrate on My presence. Do not look around you in terror and be dismayed, for I am with you. I will strengthen and harden you to difficulties. Yes, I will help you.

Those who strive against you shall be as nothing and shall perish. Though you may walk in the midst of trouble, I revive you. Watch how My right hand saves you as I stretch it forth against the wrath of every enemy to save you because you are My heart's delight.

Nothing is impossible to Me, and therefore you have nothing to be intimidated about. Speak the truth to yourself as I have shown you. The Holy Spirit guides you into the truth which lasts forever: Take the truth as your daily breath, your guide, your life. It is *true* that I will accomplish, finish and perfect everything in life that concerns you. My mercy and lovingkindness endure without shaking forever and ever.

You can do all things through Me because I continually strengthen and enable you. You can be confident, ready for anything and equal to any challenge through Me, because I continually infuse inner strength into you. You are sufficient in My sufficiency.

Though the way may be difficult to you,
it is *never* impossible.

Acts 18:10; Isaiah 41:11; Psalm 138:7, 8; John 16:13; Philippians 4:13

When Things Look Impossible

Not by might, nor by power, but by my
spirit, saith the Lord of hosts.

(Zech. 4:6, KJV)

Dear one, do not fear the task before you. Do not fear the threat of loss or disgrace or failure. There are no such descriptions in My kingdom. Perfect love casts them out.

Be confident of this very thing, that the Father, who has begun a wonderful and good work in you will continue to work it in you and through you until He sends Me to the earth again to gather up My children.

Your heavenly Father never leaves a job half done, never walks away from a thing He has originated, leaving it unfinished.

I am the Alpha and Omega,
the beginning and the end.
I am all together perfect.
My dealings with you are perfect.

I cause you to prosper in all you do.

When you drink in my word and keep it in your mind continually, meditating on it day and night to observe and do according to all that is written in it, then you shall make your way prosperous, and then you shall deal wisely and have good success. I will cause you to prosper as your soul prospers.

Nothing is impossible to Me.

Philippians 1:6; Joshua 1:8

When Your Temper Gets the Best of You

Cease from anger and forsake wrath; fret not yourself; it tends only to evil-doing.
(Ps. 37:8, Amp. Bible)

I am the author of your emotions. I love your emotions. But anger keeps you from the sweet righteousness of God.

I give you the right to experience the emotion of anger. Yet, do not sin; do not ever let your wrath, your exasperation, your fury or indignation *continue.* By allowing anger to remain in your heart, you invite Satan to influence your reasoning as well as the choices you make. I tell you, give no opportunity to him.

An unruly, selfish heart produces foul, polluted language, evil words and unwholesome, worthless talk. I have called you a child of light, which means you reflect My light. Your heavenly Father is the Maker of light. You are called to walk as a child of light and lead a life of holy wisdom. Walk in goodness, uprightness of heart and refrain from all appearances of evil.

There is no good thing in an uncontrolled temper. Do not delude or deceive yourself with empty excuses and groundless arguments for sin. A volatile temper destroys and tears down.

Fill your mind with the things that are true, honest, just, pure, lovely and of good report. My peace garrisons your heart, so above all else, guard your heart and your affections, for they influence everything in your life.

James 1:20; Ephesians 4:26, 27; Philippians 4:8, 7; Proverbs 4:23

# Instead of
Anger . . .

Do not be afraid of happiness. Happy are the people whose God is the Lord.

Do not choose to be a fool. You can release that grip of anger from you and find a happy heart. Anger has never made you wise; it has made a fool of you. Anger has never brought you blessings. Anger has never given you what you want. Your angry words have not brought forth life.

When you choose the wisdom and beauty of a pure heart, your ways become pleasing to Me. When your ways please Me, I make even your enemies to be at peace with you.

When I think of you, I do not think of you raging senselessly, but I see you greatly rejoicing in your Lord and Savior. I see you clothed in the garments of salvation and covered in the robe of righteousness, just as a bride adorns herself with jewels.

Your anger is not creative. Frustration is not inspired behavior. Anxiety is not worthy of praise. Bitterness satisfies nothing. It leaves you wanting and desolate.

Anger only breeds more anger.
But if you'll let Me,
I will put new desires in your heart.
I will put My words in your mouth
and cover you with the shadow of My hand.
I will teach you the paths of wisdom.
I will give you insight into My ways and
purposes.

Outbursts of temper are not wise and neither is an irritable spirit. The wise heart understands. And only when your heart is wise is My heart glad.

Psalm 144:15; Proverbs 18:21; 16:7; Psalm 107:9; Isaiah 50:4; 51:16; Proverbs 4:11; 23:15

When You Need Patience

In your patience possess ye your souls.
(Luke 21:19, KJV)

When I hold you in My arms, you are safe from the cruel effects of a hostile environment. My arms hold you now and you are perfectly safe.

The world you wish to control will never surrender itself to you. You cannot control your world, or the workings of your church, or the behaviors and choices of your loved ones. You cannot control the evils of life, or its injustices. *And you cannot control Me.*

But I give you the glorious privilege to know My ways and trust Me. I have all things in perfect order, on the Father's perfect time clock. Let Me love you, let Me soothe and ease your tense, impatient heart. Every concern, worry, fear, doubt and impatient thought is important to Me.

Only when you yield your thoughts to Mine am I able to communicate

My peace
and remove the discontent
from your impatient heart.

Philippians 4:6–8

# Choose

Your emotions, reasoning and decisions
depend on your choices.

You have need of patience.
you have need of peace.
Expect and believe that I am in control.
You can be assured that the Lord
lifts the head of His children
high above their enemies.

Seek My peace and My wisdom.
Inquire and require My presence.
My heart says to you,
take the authority of My Word.
Choose.

Commit your cares,
  your life,
    and your world to Me.

Hebrews 10:36

When Patience Seems Impossible

Do not, therefore, fling away your fearless
confidence, for it carries a great and
glorious compensation of reward.
(Heb. 10:35, Amp. Bible)

Steadfast patience and endurance may seem impossible to attain in the flurry of life and the pressures around you. But endurance accomplishes the Father's will and leads toward receiving and enjoying His promises to the full.

Patience may be difficult to attain at times, but it is never impossible with Me. Patience is never impossible, just as love is not impossible. You need not grind your teeth and wring your hands when things go wrong. Expect Me to be there with you. Ask yourself what your Savior thinks about the situation. My Spirit imparts to you My very thoughts.

Know that everything concerning you and your life is on schedule.

You're not too old.

It's not too late.

You haven't missed your opportunity in life.

And I am not late,

or forgetful,

or unfair.

I do not withhold blessings from you. I know exactly where you are and what your needs are. In My divine order of things, right at this moment, you are in the best place you could possibly be. Will you make something wonderful out of it? Will you glorify your Lord Jesus?

Hebrews 10:36; Psalm 27:8,14; Joshua 13:1; Psalm 31:15

Your Peace of Mind

Peace I leave with you, My peace I give to you.
                                    (John 14:27, NKJV)

It is the person with a proud heart who pounds his fists and cries, "I *want*, and I want *now!*"

Do not be quick to be angry or vexed. For anger and vexation lodge in the bosom of fools, and I save you from such things.

I give you the sweet privilege of taking My power to walk after the dictates of the Spirit, not after the dictates of the flesh.

Your peace of mind is important to Me. Peace of mind is My divine nature. Because you now have a new nature, My nature, you are a new person in Me. You are endowed with a patient heart.

So train your heart to control your desires. Know that it is never too late to change, to hope, to trust what is unseen; to wait with patience and composure for the visible effects of your prayers.

I answer you lovingly because you are precious to Me, and I remind you that the patient in spirit are of more value to Me than the proud in spirit.

Let me assure you, dear one, that I am your friend, your closest friend, and all things in your life, indeed *all* things—are working together, fitting into a plan, for *good* because you love Me and are called according to My purpose and design.

This is your peace of mind.

Ecclesiastes 7:8; Romans 8:1–28.

Allowing Yourself to Change

The [Holy] Spirit . . . intercedes and pleads
[before God] in behalf of the saints.
        (Rom. 8:27, Amp. Bible)

Give your impatient struggles to Me! Give Me
the right to be in control of all things.
    I shall change
        and renew your strength and power.
You shall be lifted up on giant wings
    and mounted close to God,
        as eagles mount up to the sun.
You shall run and not be weary;
    you shall walk and never faint,
        nor even tire.
    When you wait on Me, when you expect, look for
and hope in Me, you will find an amazing thing take
place within your heart. *You change.* Where you once
were impatient, short of temper, riddled with

frustration and nervous anxiety, you find yourself at peace. You trust Me!

As this change occurs, you no longer fret yourself because of evildoers who prosper. You no longer cry out for justice and gnash your teeth at the wickedness of the world. This change within you is sweet and glorious. You take your honored position as a child of God who has My ear, and you confidently pray in the power of My spirit

knowing

trusting

believing

resting

in the promise of My answer.

This change in you is brought by My Spirit.
Rest in me.

Wait.

Steady yourself.

Look for Me in all things, for in patience, you possess your soul.

Isaiah 40:31; Psalm 37:9; Philippians 1:6;
1 Thessalonians 5:24; Luke 21:19

When Your Faith Becomes Lukewarm

O Ephraim, what shall I do with you? [says the Lord] O Judah, what shall I do with you? For your [wavering] love and kindness are as the night mist or as the dew that goes early away.

(Hosea 6:4, Amp. Bible)

I long for you.

I long for your full heart, not just part of it.

I long for you as a friend, a close friend.

I want your total attention.

You cannot escape My thoughts,

and My longing for you never ceases.

The love songs you sang to me in the past

still echo in My ears, and your prayers,

which moved mountains,

go on bearing fruit

even without you. . . .

How many golden conversations have we shared!
    And how beautiful is your face when it is turned
    toward the Source of your life and hope!
I miss you, My friend, My little one.
    I long to show you new delights,
        new challenges,
            new insights into My written Word,
                new joys and victories.
I am not a halfway Savior. I am a total Savior.
    I saved you from defeat and death.
        I have conquered sin.
        I have conquered Satan.
I am Lord of lords and King of kings.
    My glory is indisputable, indomitable.
        I am omniscient, omnipresent and omnipotent.
        And I do not want a halfway friend.
I want you totally.

Romans 12:1; Colossians 3:17; Revelations 3:15–16

Too Busy

He has showed you, O man, what is good.
And what does the Lord require of you?
(Micah 6:8, NIV)

Becoming busy in My kingdom can make My servants too busy for Me.

Serving Me can bring about pressures you cannot handle in your human strength and talent. And My servants can flog the air for answers.

But I am here, waiting for your call. I wait for all of your heart, not just part of it.

Oh, lukewarm, storm-tossed and cast-down! All of heaven yearns for you. We rejoice over you. Have you forgotten how to dance to the heartbeat of heaven? Do you not hear the music of the angels who continually sing? You set your face like a stone and search the world for a moment of pleasure. You are neither hot nor cold. You are dissatisfied.

In *My* presence are the pleasures you crave. Dear friend, why are you cast down? Come and praise Me, let Me show you the delight of My very countenance.

Do you not know that just one glance toward My splendor would revitalize your lagging spirit and send your hopes soaring? Do you not remember it is I who have the power to transform?

Come back to My heart,

come running back!

Do not look around in dismay any longer,

for I am your God.

Let our hearts again rejoice in the sunlight of our friendship and I will help you. Yes! I will hold you up and sustain you with My victorious right hand.

Come back.

Psalm 42:5, 6, 11; Isaiah 41:10

When You Need Strength

*My soul is weary with sorrow; strengthen
me according to your word.*
(Psalm 119:28, NIV)

Child of mine, greatly beloved, fear not. I am
with you to calm your fears. Be strong. When your
Lord tells you to be strong, it is because you have My
strength within you to draw upon.

Raging, or running to and fro in panic will erode
your energy and rob your vitality. You need strength
in your body as well as your spirit. I grant you,
according to the riches of My glory, to be strengthened
with might by My Spirit in the inner chambers of your
being.

I am your rock.

I am your fortress.

I am your deliverer.

I am your strength.

Sadness of heart will sap your strength. Watch

over your heart with all diligence, reminding yourself I am your light and your salvation.

You have nothing to fear. I am the strength of your life.

What can you fear?

You are strong

because I am strong.

Daniel 10:19; Ephesians 3:16; Psalm 18:2; Ephesians 6:19

Growing Stronger

Have you not known? Have you not heard? The everlasting God, the Lord, the Creator of the ends of the earth, does not faint or grow weary.

(Isa. 40:28, Amp. Bible)

Lift up your eyes, dear one. Who has created you? You were formed by a master technician, an artist from whom all art and beauty evolves. You were formed perfectly by the Source of all life. There is no way to fathom the understanding of the Lord.

I give power to you when you feel faint. When you have no might I increase your strength. I cause your strength to multiply and I bring joy to your spirit causing strength and might to abound in you. All strength is Mine. I give you more strength than you are able to manifest in your human ability. I give you more energy than that of the skilled athlete who competes in the contest of champions. I give you all the strength you need for this moment of your life.

In the past you have worried you would weary in your labors. You made provision for impending tiredness and lack of strength. You told those around you that you expected little strength.

I tell you, and it is a certainty, *I give you My strength.*

In Me, you have strength of character, spiritual strength and physical strength. In Me your mind is alive and alert. Your thoughts are sound, because they are born of a steadfast heart.

You were once a slave to sin and weakness.

Sin's diseases were in your thoughts and deeds. But now you are clean through My word
which I have spoken to you.
My blood cleanses you
and I blot out your sins.

Don't call up past sins. Don't dig them out of the forgiven past and walk in them again. You are My righteousness now. I strengthen you day by day. This strengthening is continual, as you are daily delivered from sin's dominion.

Glory in your freedom in Me, and rejoice with Me every day. My joy is your strength.

Psalm 139:13–16; Isaiah 40:29; Romans 6:17; 5:10; John 15:3; 1 John 1:9; Nehemiah 8:10

Your Weakness— My Strength

My Strength is made perfect in weakness.
(2 Cor. 12:9, KJV)

Why do you need strength? Are you weary?
Do you have a heavy burden, too heavy for your own
shoulders and your own emotion?

I know your needs. My grace is sufficient to fill
every need. My grace, My unmerited favor, is *all* you
need.

There is an enemy of strength. There is an enemy
who keeps you from understanding My Word: "Let
the weak say I am strong."

Are you your own enemy?
An enemy is one
    who keeps you from My best for you.
An enemy is one
    who robs you of eternal joy
    and gladness of heart
    by withholding the truth

from you.

An enemy is one

whose sole desire is to pull curses from your lips against your Holy, heavenly Father.

Yes, you are weak. You cannot stand against the devil, the enemy of God. Your flesh is weak even when it is strong. Your flesh has no power over this enemy of God.

I came to this world to destroy the work of the devil. Sin is the seed of weakness, and it reaps more weakness.

But in your weakness I make you strong. I have said it. I have breathed strength into you by My Spirit.

My strength and power are made perfect in your weakness.

2 Corinthians 12:9; 1 John 3:8

Your Weakness Is Your Pathway to Strength

For thou hast been a strength to the poor, a
strength to the needy in his distress.
(Isa. 25:4, KJV)

Many servants of Mine have gone before you,
  and as weak vessels
    they extinguished the power of raging fire,
      escaped the devourings of the sword,
  and in their frailty and weakness
    won My strength
    and became stalwart
      and mighty in battle.
Rejoice and glory that in your human, fleshly self
  you are weak.
Glory in these weaknesses and infirmities
  because the strength and power of your Lord
  will fill, cover, and dwell upon you

to make you more than a conqueror.

Your natural weakness is your path to spiritual strength, because in your human frailty, My strength is more than sufficient against any danger. I enable you to bear all troubles as a warrior.

My strength and power are fulfilled
    and completed
        and show themselves most effective
    in your weakness.

Since you desire and seek proof of My power within you,
    realize I am not weak
        and feeble
            in My dealing with you.
    I am a mighty power within you.

The only time you are weak, My child,
    is when you choose to live
        in your own strength,
    not Mine.

I give you the power
    to live in radiant intensity of joy
    and power and enthusiasm
        at the highest level of My Spirit's ability.

From this moment on

refer to weakness not as an enemy,
for weakness opens the way to My power.

Hebrews 11:34; Romans 8:37;
2 Corinthians 12:9, 10; 13:3

When Weariness Overtakes You

As for you, brethren, do not be weary or
lose heart in doing right [but continue in
well-doing without weakening].
(2 Thess. 3:13, Amp. Bible)

Why has your life suddenly lost its zeal?

Are your hands hanging limply at your sides? Is that your voice sighing in the night and whispering furtively in the darkness, "I don't care anymore"?

But you *do* care! You *do* have deep and intense interests!

Your rewards, however, have been few. Hope deterred makes the heart sick. It is not that rewards have not been waiting for you, because when desire is fulfilled it is a tree of life.

I am your life.

In Me, you create your rewards. But you have been misled in waiting for others to reward you. I have told you not to be weary in well-doing.

There is a weariness resulting from wrong-doing, but why do you weary in that which pleases Me?

Genesis 15:1; Proverbs 13:12; Galatians 6:9

Beyond the Gates of Grace

It is vain for you to rise up early, to take rest
late, to eat the bread of [anxious] toil; for He
gives [blessing] to His beloved in sleep.
(Ps. 127:2, Amp. Bible)

I never sulk, but you are sulking.
I never pout, but you are pouting.

I never complain, or shrink from the light. But look
at you. You are tired. I am not.

You are precious to Me and altogether beautiful in
your godly splendor.

For I have created you and formed you in My
image
    to draw you into My heart
    and share not only My likeness
    but My thoughts.
You were created
    to reflect the Father,
        and to please Him.

If you are weary
and your soul is heavy,
have you pressed yourself
beyond the gates of grace?
And do you seek strength in places I am not?
Turn from Me
to eat the bread of anxious toil
and instantly you grow weary.
Do My pleasure
in the energy of My joy,
and your body, soul and spirit
will soar like the eagle.
My desire is that you make your bed in the
stars
above the cares of the world,
not in the mud.

Isaiah 40:28–31; Nehemiah 8:10; Ephesians 1:19–23;
Colossians 3:1, 2

Exchanging Your Weariness for Rewards

But thanks be to God, Who in Christ always leads
us in triumph—as trophies of Christ's victory.
(2 Cor. 2:14, Amp. Bible)

Draw near to My heart and enter into My presence and see Me for who I am—Believe that I am the rewarder and I reward you. Nothing that you do in My name goes unnoticed by Me.

It may seem that others get the rewards and I forget you, but this is not true. Exchange your weary thoughts for thoughts of hope and truth. Exchange your pessimistic, gloomy thoughts, which expect evil and calamity, for My mind. You limit yourself when you allow weariness to give way to self-pity.

I give you everything you need; I give you heart-peace. What greater reward is there than that? It passes human understanding. It is beyond carnal skills.

I soothe you, comfort you. Let Me ease your troubled, weary mind. In all situations, at all times, I am with you.

Hebrews 11:6; John 14:27; Matthew 28:20

Avoid Weariness of the Soul

Unless your law had been my delight, I would have perished in my affliction.
(Ps. 119:92, Amp. Bible)

You are blessed by Me. I tell you to rejoice and be exceedingly glad that you are mine, for great is your reward in heaven.

The prophets were persecuted before you and even in this day My children are persecuted. In your suffering you reign with Me.

But avoid the weariness that results from sin.

It wastes the soul

and burns your energy like brittle leaves.

Do not lose heart, My dear one,

Do not faint in good and noble deeds

done in the name of your Savior,

for in My time, which is always perfect,

and at the appointed season,

you shall reap

rewards more glorious
than the eye has seen or the ear has
heard.
I promise.

Matthew 5:11, 12; 2 Timothy 2:12

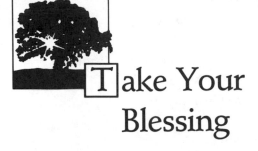

Take Your Blessing

Return to your rest, O my soul, for the
Lord has dealt bountifully with you.
(Ps. 116:7, Amp. Bible)

Do not allow your courage to unravel
  and be scattered.
Think about and meditate on your rewards.
  Your thoughts are at the core of your heart.

I see you in your glorious crown,
  which will never fade nor tarnish.
    For under trial,
  you stand firm
and when tempted to become weary,
  you stand the test and see your rewards.
Offer yourself willingly to Me
  in My power
    in the beauty of holiness
      and in holy array.

Come to Me like dew
in the stillness of the morning.

For I do not allow My righteous ones to famish
and the treasures of My heart
will bless you in every trial.

This is the instruction
that multiplies your days:
Be wise.
Exchange your weariness for my rewards.
My blessings are upon your head,
the fruit of which is better than gold,
yes, more than refined gold,
and My increase is better than choice silver.
Take.

Galatians 6:9; James 1:12; Psalm 110:3; Proverbs 10:3;
9:11; 10:6; 8:19

The Deceiver

Be sober, be vigilant; because your adversary
the devil, as a roaring lion, walketh
about, seeking whom he may devour.
(1 Pet. 5:8, KJV)

Oh My child, do not let outward appearances deceive you. Do not allow yourself to be as a plaything for the devil, untrained for battle, undisciplined in your affections and emotions.

Do not be ignorant of the devices of the devil. He roams about like a lion in fierce hunger, ever hunting for a human being to seize upon and devour. The devil blinds the children of the world with hideous deceptions designed to mutilate and destroy all that is lovely and good.

Withstand this evil one.

Be firm in faith

and grow strong roots;

become established and unmovable in Me.

You are not alone, so be bold to tell the world

you belong to Me!

You are Mine. Your enemy knows that and he trembles.

But dear one, you must put aside naive interpretations of who I am and what I do, and trust in My written Word.

I want you to prosper and be in good health.

I want your soul to grow strong.

I want you to be overtaken and overwhelmed
    with blessings!

        But the devil will steal

        anything he can get from you.

        In cunning hatred

        he claws, chews, lies, roars

        and assaults in order to kill.

Be ready.

    Be alert.

        Be wise.

Stay close to Me.

2 Corinthians 2:11; 1 Peter 5:8, 9; James 2:19; 3 John 2;
1 Corinthians 16:13

God Is a Giver

Now we have not received the spirit (that belongs to) the world, but the (Holy) Spirit Who is from God, [given to us] that we might realize and comprehend and appreciate the gifts (of divine favor and blessing so freely and lavishly) bestowed on us by God.
(1 Cor. 2:12, Amp. Bible)

It is My will that you behave wisely and prosper in all you do. And by keeping My words in your heart and *doing* them, you will prosper.

I am a giving God!

When you listen diligently to My voice,

when you obey, love, and press tightly

into My love for you,

I lift you up above all cares of the world.

When you thrill to My voice

and respond as a sheep to its shepherd,

blessings will rain upon you!

I want you blessed everywhere your foot
steps,
whether city or field.
This blessing I speak of is everlasting. It will not
end when your life on earth is through. This blessing
is beyond what the eye sees and the ear hears.
I give you
the priceless treasure of faith in My abilities
and in My love for you,
a tranquil heart in the midst of trouble and
despair,
quietness and confidence in the face of
danger.
I give you
strength and courage beyond your natural
potential,
wisdom and understanding,
contentment in all things.
I give you a new nature and a new mind, and this
blessing is so great you will never be able to exhaust
its endless outpouring. And what greater blessing is
there than a happy heart? Happiness is produced by
knowing My favor and matchless grace, regardless of
outward conditions.
Never let yourself believe My blessings are only

material or that I am limited to your prayers. I give you far more than you ask when I give you a new heart.

Romans 14:17; 2 Corinthians 4:16–17

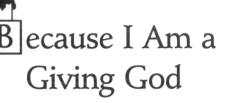

Because I Am a Giving God

Yes, the Lord will give what is good.
(Ps. 85:12, Amp. Bible)

Because I am a giving God and I love you,
  to you, My child, who pleases Me,
  I give wisdom and knowledge and joy!

Because I am a giving God, and I love you,
  I bring you to a place of great joy.
  I meet all your needs.
  I keep you safe and blessed
    in a place where you lack no good thing.

Because I am a giving God and I love you,
  I have given you the secret knowledge
  of the mysteries of the kingdom of heaven.
  And because you choose My Spirit,
    and a life in Me,
more will be given to you.

Because you are My friend, and you hear My words
    and grasp them,
        you are richly furnished.

Because you receive,
    I freely give.

Ecclesiastes 2:26; Deuteronomy 8:7–9; Philippians 4:19;
Matthew 13:11–13, 23

As You Receive, Give

Bear ye one another's burdens, and so fulfil
the law of Christ.
(Gal. 6:2, KJV)

I have given you the Holy Spirit. Not a spirit belonging to the world, but the Holy Spirit who is from God.

My Holy Spirit gives you beautiful understanding and appreciation of My gifts, divine favor and blessing, which I so freely and lavishly give to you.

These are the gifts you give to others. And the greatest gift you can give is the reflection you bear of Me.

In My *wisdom*, you shine brightly
and turn many to righteousness.
The gift of *truth* is without price,
which you give freely
to all who have ears to hear.
You shall serve the Lord your God in all your

ways. You will love your enemies, and be kind and do good.

Hope for nothing in return for your good and loving deeds, and I will reward you richly and abundantly.

You are a child of the Most High,
so be merciful as I am merciful to you;
sympathetic as I am sympathetic to you,
tender as I am tender to you,
responsive as I respond to you,
and compassionate as I have compassion on you.

You are born of Me and so your gift to me and to your world, is to walk as I would walk.

I am in your shoes.

1 Corinthians 2:12; Daniel 12:3; Luke 6:35

The Thankful Heart

Enter his gates with thanksgiving and his
courts with praise; give thanks to him . . .
                    (Ps. 100:4, NIV)

My little one, I am delivering you from sadness and gloomy introspection. Allow Me to draw you to the glorious place of gladness and celebration in My Spirit.

For I have taken you out of the control and dominion of darkness. I have transferred you into My kingdom of the Father's perfect and marvelous love.

Your daily breath and constantly growing knowledge of My will makes you glad. Can you not feel the glory of thankfulness well up within you?

Is My spiritual wisdom and understanding not enough for you?

Rejoice in thankfulness.
Lean your entire personality on Me
    and give thanks!

Colossians 1:13; 1:9, 10–12

The Language of
a Thankful Heart

*Thank [God] in everything—no matter what the
circumstances may be, be thankful and give
thanks; for this is the will of God for you . . .*
(1 Thess. 5:18, Amp. Bible)

The language of thanksgiving
is the language of glory.
The quality of praise transcends
all things base and earthly.
The Father has given My life to you,
and the blood which poured from My body
redeems you,
offers you forgiveness,
new life,
sweetness of soul,
sleep without terror
and joy unspeakable.
Is this not reason to be thankful?

Colossians 1:14

The Power of Thankfulness

Through Him therefore let us constantly and at
all times offer up to God a sacrifice of praise.
(Heb. 13:15, Amp. Bible)

Cherish thankfulness. Know that even now you
are partaking of the same joyous experience of angels,
who surround the throne of God in multitudes,
giving thanks to the Lord God Almighty,
who is and was and will be to come!
Let thankfulness, My dearest child, constantly and
at all times, gush upward to Me in a sacrifice of praise.

Let your thankful heart be your good friend. I tell
you, because I love you, to constantly make thanksgiving the language in which you think and speak.
Then, when you are tempted to be cast down, the
feeling will be blown from your spirit like dust.

In all circumstances, let the treasure of your
thankful heart rule your Spirit.

See how strong your heart grows in thankfulness,

for I give you very great cause to be thankful.
I will in no way fail you,
    neither will I in any way forsake you.
We are together forever.

Hebrews 13:15; Genesis 28:15; Deuteronomy 31:6;
Joshua 1:5

The Song of the Thankful Heart

And He has put a new song in my mouth,
a song of praise to our God.
(Ps. 40:3, Amp. Bible)

Thank the Father, and be thankful in all things,
for this is His will concerning you!

Caress and tightly hold the knowledge that,
though your soul wrestle
    with the dragons of hell,
    and you walk among the lions,
        I am exalted in you.

I reward you
    and perform for good on your behalf,
        always bringing to pass My purposes for you.

Sing from a thankful heart,
    and I sing with you.

1 Thessalonians 5:18; Isaiah 46:10, 11

The Song of God

Yet the Lord will command His loving-kindness in the daytime, and in the night His song shall be with me, a prayer to the God of my life.

(Ps. 42:8, Amp. Bible)

When you feel tempted to discouragement,
give Me praise.

I am the help of your countenance,
    the water for your thirst.
        Lift up your voice,
            even in the smallest strains,
                and sing.

Rise up on the wings of prayer, My beloved,
    and let the song I have born in you arise;
and you will hear My voice
    in harmony with yours.

Come sing with Me,
   come dance with Me,
      in joy and jubilation,
   for I have dealt lovingly with you.

Psalm 13:6

S ing

I will sing to the Lord as long as I live; I will
sing praise to my God while I have any being.
(Ps. 104:33, Amp. Bible)

When you are prisoned in your hour of pain,
        sing.
When you are captured by sorrow,
        sing.
When the chains of disappointment cut your flesh,
    and your heart is wilted with anguish,
    and your eyes form wells of tears,
        sing.

    I have not taught you to sing only when you
are happy and free from troubles. I have shown you
that the turmoils of life cannot defeat you.
Sit upon the strength of My shoulders
        and sing!

When You Are Irritable

*He has not dealt with us after our sins, nor
rewarded us according to our iniquities.*
(Ps. 103:10, Amp. Bible)

You are precious to Me
    even when you are irritable.
And when you angrily curl your lip
    against the day,
I love you.
When you curse the dawn,
    and the gifts I've given you,
I still love you.
    I do not faint in shock.
I am never shaken.
Though I demand holiness,
    I do not condemn you,
        even when you're irritable,
        and unlovely to yourself.
    For I have delivered your soul, and I release you

from the deception that grows in your heart like mold
on a rotting piece of fruit.

I redeem your life from the pit
and beautify you with mercy.

For I do not deal with you after your sins, My
child. I do not reward you according to iniquity. And
though you are irritable for a moment, you will return,
and in our sweet communion you will again be
satisfied.

In My loving kindness,
you can be at peace with
your many moods.

Psalm 17:7, 8; 103:4, 10; Isaiah 7:15

The Melancholy Heart

Therefore remove [the lusts that end in] sorrow and vexation from your heart and mind, and put away evil from your body.
(Eccles. 11:10, Amp. Bible)

I am aware of the pestilence of soul that stalks the darkness and the destructive melancholy that wastes the noon and I tell you: Do not lose your vision.

Your need for Me is far greater than the portion of Me you take. When even the smallest things become a burden and you are annoyed at specks and grasshoppers, return to My heart, which never waxes old or tired.

Remember your Creator. Know that you are not your own, but His property.

Those who have walked a lifetime without My Spirit meet the gathering of their years with discontent and find no pleasure in the days and nights. The sin of gloom is the foundation of the walls of hell.

But you. You do not walk in the disabling shadows of a hungry, barren spirit. You command your soul with authority to bless the Lord.

And I will be blessed by you.

Psalm 91:6; Ecclesiastes 12:1, 6

Bless the Lord

*Bless—affectionately, gratefully praise—
the Lord, O my soul, and all that is
[deepest] within me, bless His holy name!*
(Ps. 103:1, Amp. Bible)

When you command your soul to bless the Lord,
    to affectionately and gratefully praise Me
        with all that is deepest within you,
My benefits are released to you.
Your life is redeemed from the pit of corruption,
    you are beautified and dignified,
        crowned with lovingkindness and tender
        mercies.
Your necessities are met
    and your youth renewed like the eagle's!
You are again strong.
    You are an overcomer.
        You soar!

Psalm 103:1–5

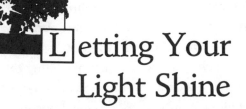

Letting Your Light Shine

Turn not aside from following the Lord, but
serve Him with all your heart; and turn not
aside after vain and worthless things which
cannot profit or deliver you, for they are
empty and futile.
(1 Sam. 12:20–21, Amp. Bible)

You were created to bring beauty and healing
to a world lying locked in the clutches of a perpetual
throbbing curse.

The voices of hell screech at the children of the
world day and night. And in this invisible realm, all
choices are influenced.

But you,

shining as the sun in beauty and brightness,

are born of My Spirit.

You refute the ugly curses. You are not swallowed
by the lies. And in the majesty of My truth, by the
glorious will of the loving Father,

healing is released
through your prayers.

If you desire to be a blessing, to bring help to someone in despair, concentrate on the Source of blessing, on the One who is the Helper.

There is much fear and alarm surrounding the sickbed of a dying world. And when you draw near to pray do not allow your eye or your emotions to be your guide,
but fix your mind on My presence
and your light will shine.

Hebrews 12:2; 13:5, 6 (Amp. Bible)

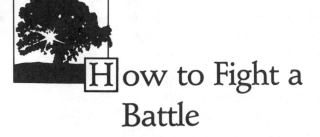

How to Fight a Battle

*For the weapons of our warfare are not
physical (weapons of flesh and blood), but
they are mighty before God.*
(2 Cor. 10:4, Amp. Bible)

You never need worry when you face a battle,
dear one, because you will always win if I am at the
lead.

I will go before you
    and you will overthrow
        and destroy strongholds.

But not with the tools of human warfare according
to the flesh—mere human weapons. I would have you
remember that in battle you are not wrestling with
flesh and blood, contending only with physical
opponents. Your real battle is against the spiritual
powers who rule the darkness. Your war is against
spirit forces of wickedness in the supernatural sphere.

Your kind of battle requires My complete armor

which you must wear in order to resist and stand your ground. Your belt, breastplate, boots, shield, helmet and sword are vital battle attire and dispensed only by Me.

You win all battles by standing
in the power of truth
and righteousness
with firm-footed stability.
You win your battle
by skillfully wielding
the sword of the Spirit,
which is My Word.

My Word is alive and full of power. It is sharper than any two-edged sword. When you wield My Word, consuming flames fly.

My Word is like a hammer
that crushes and breaks rocks into pieces.
Oh, My soldier,
with My perfect armor,
you are more than a conqueror.

2 Chronicles 20:15, 17, 20; 2 Corinthians 10:4;
Ephesians 6:10–18; Hebrews 4:12; Romans 8:37

When the Enemies Come at You

O God, the proud are risen against me, and the assemblies of violent men have sought after my soul.

(Ps. 86:14, KJV)

I tell you, My mighty one, and it is the truth, you shall not be overcome and trampled underfoot by your enemies.

Put on your armor *before* the battle and the arrows will not reach your flesh.

The fight of faith is not a bad fight; it is a good fight. Because no soldier of God, when in battle, becomes entangled in the vanity of worldly care. The soldier's aim is to honor and satisfy the One who sent him.

You cannot afford to keep company with worry, My beloved. As Goliath of old approached my young servant, David, with brawling confidence, so does your enemy, Satan, approach you.

Respond as David did, with resounding, clarion voice,

"So! You come at me with a sword, only a spear, and only a shield, but I come to you in the name of the Lord of hosts!"
I shall cause your enemies
>   who rise up against you
>>   to be defeated before your face;
>>>   they shall come out against you one way,
>>>>   and flee before you seven ways.
>   Express yourself in Me.

Ephesians 6:10–18; 1 Timothy 6:12; 2 Timothy 2:4; 1 Samuel 17:45; Deuteronomy 28:7

Ending Your War with Others

A soft answer turns away wrath.
(Prov. 15:1, Amp. Bible)

There is a way which has seemed right to you in the past, but the end of it is death.

Do not let it surprise you when a child of Mine behaves unseemly, for it is bound to be your experience. But I do not want you to take an eye for an eye. If a brother or sister strikes you on the face, turn your other cheek. Do not strike back.

Indeed, you have initiated foolish battles that never needed to be fought. You have jumped forward, swinging both fists at the mere whisper of opposition.

Be slow to anger, dear one, and show your depth of understanding at these times, because when you are hasty of spirit, you expose and exalt folly.

Your brother and sister are not your enemies; your enemy is the devil.

He stalks about looking for someone to devour.

He leers from behind every corner,
>   waiting to expose folly and foolishness
>   in My children.
Wisdom rests quietly
>   in the mind and heart of My chosen ones
>   who have developed understanding.

Make peace with those whom you have been at odds with. Hold your peace and be at rest. If there is a battle to be fought, I'll fight it for you.

For there will come a day when you will long that those you have made enemies of, will be your friends. There will come a day when you will lament slaying with your tongue the righteous ones. For if you wage war against your own brother or sister, whom shall I send to protect them against you?

Be gentle, My little one, and if a brother or a sister has a difference or a grievance with you, readily pardon, even as I freely forgive you. Your true fellowship is with your brothers and sisters because you are living and walking in the light.

My blood cleanses and removes all sin and guilt in order that you may truly love.

Proverbs 4:12; 14:29, 33; Exodus 14:14; 1 John 1:7; 4:7

The Refiner's Fire

For He is like a refiner's fire and like fullers' soap.
He will sit as a refiner and purifier of silver.
(Mal. 3:2,3, Amp. Bible)

Do not be amazed when you face the refiner's fire, for it is a good thing.

In My house there are vessels of gold and silver, but there are also utensils of wood and earthenware. Some of these are for honorable and noble use and some for menial use.

Cleanse yourself from what is ignoble and unclean; separate yourself from contact with contaminating and corrupting influences.

I would have you as a vessel set apart,

beautiful and useful

for honorable, noble, godly purposes.

I would have you fit and ready

for the Master's use.

You are in need of refinement

like gold and silver.
Therefore wash your hands and purify your heart.

You are My child,
    ordained to resemble
        and be like Me.
Do not remain in communion with evil,
    because wisdom is pure.
My Holy Spirit will purify you
    and the refiner's fire will not sting
If you are glad in heart
    to see the evil influences
        washed from your mind.

2 Timothy 2:20–21; 1 John 3:2; James 3:17

The Pure Heart Is a Refined One

*And every one who has this hope [resting]
on Him cleanses (purifies) himself just as
He is pure—chaste, undefiled, guiltless.*
(1 John 3:3, Amp. Bible)

To the pure in heart and conscience, all things are pure, but to the defiled and corrupt nothing is pure.

This refining may take several forms. It may be a no from Me on some very simple request. It may ask you to give up some habits that you have clung to like a toy. I may remove you from a place to which you've grown attached.

In order to worship your Lord in the beauty of holiness, you must trust Me completely, for I want you to realize My sovereignty.

Allow Me My free will.

At the root of your disappointment,

I am there.

At the root of unmerited rebuke,
    I am there.
At the center of the unexpected hardship,
    I am there.
    I want you trained by My Spirit,
refined in every respect,
      so you can always find a star
        in the blackest night,
always discover joy in the morning,
    treasure in the midst of lack,
      and peace in the midst of the raging storm.

Hebrews 12:11; Titus 1:15

The Heart of Faith

Now faith is being sure of what we hope for
and certain of what we do not see. This is
what the ancients were commended for. By
faith we understand that the universe was
formed at God's command, so that what is
seen was not made out of what was visible.
(Heb. 11:1-3, NIV)

Without faith it is impossible to please and be
satisfactory to Me. It is necessary for you to know in
your heart that the Father, Son and Holy Spirit are the
greatest reality.

I am the Rewarder of everyone
    who earnestly and diligently seeks Me out.
Faith is only gained through My Word.
It is a holy and blessed gift.
    Faith increases daily
        as you absorb the Word of Truth

into your soul and spirit.

If you would be just, you must live by,
    breathe by,
        eat by,
            sleep by
                faith.

Hebrews 11:6; Romans 10:17

Climb Your Mountain

*For truly, I say to you, if you have faith
[that is living] like a grain of mustard seed,
you can say to this mountain, Move from
here to yonder place, and it will move, and
nothing will be impossible to you.*
(Matt. 17:20, Amp. Bible)

Faith is the sweet realization
　　that I am your supplier of life;
　　　　that I am the Resurrection
　　　　and *all* there is.
I am the Son of God,
　　I am the King of kings,
　　　　Lord of lords.

By believing in Me you have everlasting life. You'll never die.

Faith is a magnetic spiritual force. You connect your mind to Mine and allow Me to permeate your being with a knowledge of Myself and the kingdom of

God, of which you are a citizen.
Out of you flow rivers of living water.

Through you I pour My life—*through* you—
always moving,

never stagnant, still or dull.
Saturate your mind in My word

and look unto Me,

the Author and Finisher

of your faith.

Learn to believe. For when you believe, all things
are possible to you.

This is the faith that moves mountains.

Climb.

John 11:25; 20:31; 3:16; John 7:38; Hebrews 12:2; Mark
9:23

Power to Follow

"Anyone who wants to follow me must put aside his own desires and conveniences and carry his cross with him every day and keep close to me!"

(Luke 9:23, TLB)

You have the power within you to ask what you will and it shall be done unto you. You are My disciple.

Joy and peace have begun in your heart. They continue to gather a harvest of delight as the reality of your new life takes shape. Build your life in Me. Be willing to follow Me daily,

as My disciple,

My child,

My friend.

You are growing as a baby grows. And every day My life is being formed in you.

You are discovering My way of doing things and

learning that self-denial is not a bad or a cruel thing. You are not being punished when you deny yourself the selfish indulgences you wish for.

It is not too hard to say yes to Me and My gentle nudgings. For when you abandon petty fleshly indulgences and the pursuit of self-protection, you'll know,

realize and experience

the joy and health of

being free.

My dear one, discipline is freedom.

So great is My love for you, I insist upon it.

1 John 3:1, 2; Galatians 4:19

Your Real Self

I have loved you with an everlasting love;
therefore with loving-kindness have I drawn you.
(Jer. 31:3, Amp. Bible)

You may not know, even in the abundance of
your years, how dear you are to the heart of God. Yet
you *can* fully realize the depths of riches in the Father's
heart!

My dearest,
if you would come away with Me,
and let Me love you,

I will show you My treasures,
tell you My secrets,
give you My holy and glorious gifts
and multiplied fruit!

I give you far beyond and above what you ask,
and your eye has not seen the magnificent
surprises
I have in store for you
because you love Me.

I have given you My Spirit to show you all of
God's deepest thoughts.
You are altogether lovely,
   altogether beautiful,
      and it is to you I sing My love song;
         it is to you I give My heart.

1 Corinthians 2:9, 10; Song of Solomon 4:6–10

The Gentle and Pure Heart

The Lord knows those who are His, and,
Let every one who names [himself by] the
name of the Lord give up all iniquity and
stand aloof from it.
     (2 Tim. 2:19, Amp. Bible)

Pursue that which is virtuous and good,
     the righteous and holy life,
conforming to My will in thought,
          word and deed.
Aim at harmony with other Christians,
     seek love and peace.

But shut your mind against
          trifling, ill-formed, unedifying, stupid
          controversies
that foster strife and quarreling.

     The servant of the Lord must not be quarrelsome,

189

ill-tempered, contentious. Be known by others for your mild-tempered and wise ways. Preserve the bond of peace with the family of God.

If I call you servant, you must be skilled at teaching and sharing My truth. You must be patient, forbearing and willing to suffer wrong.

Be courteous and gentle as you help others, because you know Me and you know that I am longing for others to know Me as you do.

2 Timothy 2:22–25

The Life of the Disciple

Choose you this day whom you will serve.
(Josh. 24:15, Amp. Bible)

I have made it easy for you to *receive* my love,
but the *walk* of love is not easy. It means denying
yourself, turning the other cheek, putting others'
needs before your own, bridling your selfish desires,
dying to the flesh.

The life of the disciple is separated, holy, given
entirely to Me.

Then wisdom, joy and life

like rivers of gushing waters

flow out of your innermost being.

You must understand that the godly person is
unselfish. The call of my disciple is to live for Me, not
for personal gain. For you to live is Christ.

I give you happiness and comfort in the Holy
Spirit. But the price you pay is your complete
surrender to Me and My will.

Choose today
    to love, worship and obey
        your Lord and Savior and Him only.
Choose today
    to see the Father for more
        than meeting your own personal wants and
        needs.
Choose today
    to serve Him with your whole self.
Leave your burdens,
    possessions and personal baggage
        at the entrance to the eye of the needle.
Pass through to stand before His throne of grace
    and worship!

Romans 12:1; 6:17–19